A Word A DAY
Primary

A Word a Day provides a structured format to help students build vocabulary on a daily basis. Each of the 366 lessons contains the following features:

Part of Speech
The part of speech is given for each word. Teachers may choose whether to share this information.

Contextualized Sentence
Each new word is used in context, in a sentence. Each sentence is designed to provide enough context about the new word that students can easily grasp its meaning.

Definition
Each entry word is defined with a complete sentence.

A Word a Day

abdomen

noun

The **abdomen** is the part of the body that holds the stomach, intestines, and other organs.

The scar on my **abdomen** is next to my belly button.

Which of these is part of the **abdomen**?
- your skin
- your elbow
- your navel
- your belly
- your tongue

Tell about a time when you had a pain in your **abdomen**. What caused it? What helped it feel better?

Critical Attributes
To help students better understand and articulate exactly what the new word means, these exercises require them to identify features that are and are not attributes of the target word. One of the most effective ways to help students identify subtleties of meaning is to identify attributes that do ***not*** apply.

Personal Connection
For each new word, students are asked to share an opinion, personal experience, or other comment that demonstrates their understanding of the new word. Connecting new information to previous experience facilitates learning.

How to Use

Scheduling

The one-a-day format is flexible enough to fit into your daily schedule in many ways. Consider any of the following:

- Introduce a new word each morning as part of your opening activities or other daily language activities.

- Present a new word as a warm-up activity before beginning reading and language arts instruction.

- Conduct activities as a way to provide focus during transition times.

- Photocopy pages and send them home to involve families in language development at home.

Presenting the Entries

To use the **Word a Day** activities in class, you may:

- Make overhead transparencies to present each of the new vocabulary words. Read aloud the word and its definition, as well as the contextualized sentence. You may continue to refer to the text on the overhead as you conduct the critical-attribute and personal-experience activities. This approach will be appreciated by all students who are visual learners.

- Read the entry for each word aloud to your class, and conduct the activities as strictly oral activities. In this case, you should write the word on the chalkboard so that students will have a visual association for it. This will allow both auditory and visual learners multiple ways in which to process the new information.

- If you wish to help strengthen students' ability to work in both auditory and visual modes, alternate your mode of presentation of the **Word a Day** entries.

Tips for Conducting the Activities

- When you conduct critical-attribute activities, be sure to call on different students to respond to the five choices in each exercise. By calling on students at random, you keep the lesson moving and the students engaged.

- Invite more than one student to respond to any of the five choices in the critical-attribute exercises, or to the personal-experience exercise. Ask the group if anybody came up with a different response, or had a different way of thinking about the exercise. Be sure students explain their answers or use logic to support their statements. When students explain their thinking, you or your students may learn that there is more than one way to look at any given exercise.

- Remind students to be courteous listeners, giving full attention to the speaker. When unusual or minority opinions are expressed, remind students that each person is entitled to hold his or her own opinion. Encourage students to defend their opinions with logic. (This should help unusual opinions gain acceptance.)

Creating Student Word Books

Use the patterns on pages 187 and 188 to help students create individual word books. Follow these steps:

1. Make one copy of the cover page per student, reproducing the pattern on card stock or construction paper.

2. Reproduce at least 25 copies of the entry page per student.

3. Staple or use paper fasteners to assemble pages into book form.

4. Students may write new words they wish to remember or incorporate into their spoken or written vocabulary, then write a definition, use the word in a sentence, and add an illustration when appropriate.

Students may refer to their word books to help them enrich their writing. They might also like to copy text they encounter during their reading that includes the target word.

As an additional option, students may list synonyms, antonyms, or both for the new words they learn.

A Word a Day

abdomen

noun

The **abdomen** is the part of the body that holds the stomach, intestines, and other organs.

The scar on my **abdomen** is next to my belly button.

Which of these is part of the **abdomen**?

- your skin
- your elbow
- your navel
- your belly
- your tongue

Tell about a time when you had a pain in your **abdomen**. What caused it? What helped it feel better?

clever

adjective

A **clever** person can figure things out quickly.

The **clever** toddler soon discovered how to open the safety gate.

Would you be **clever** if you

- invented a complicated machine?
- decided what to eat for breakfast?
- tried to breathe underwater?
- guessed the ending of a movie before anyone else?
- learned all your new spelling words in one day?

Describe something **clever** you have done at home. What is something **clever** you've done at school?

A Word a Day, Primary • EMC 2717 • ©2002 by Evan-Moor Corp.

dainty

adjective

Something is **dainty** when it is very delicate.

The **dainty** tea cakes crumbled when I dropped them.

Which of these is **dainty**?

- a wrestler
- a rosebud
- the lace on a baby's dress
- a fine china teacup
- an elephant

Find something **dainty** in the classroom. What is something **dainty** that you have at home?

pounce

verb

You **pounce** when you jump on something suddenly.

The deer got away before the crouching bobcat could **pounce** on it.

Which words go with **pounce**?

- leap
- sit
- stand
- jump
- sleep

Do you think it's a good idea to **pounce** on another person? Why or why not?

A Word a Day

generous

adjective

A person who is willing to share with others is **generous**.

The **generous** man shared his prize money with his friends.

Would you be **generous** if you

- shared your candy bar with a friend?
- spent your allowance on a gift for your sister?
- got a new scooter that you would not let your best friend ride?
- ate a bag of chips by yourself while your hungry friends watched?
- let someone else have the piece of your birthday cake with the rose on it?

Tell about something **generous** that someone did for you. What is something **generous** that you have done for somebody? How did it make you feel?

rambunctious

adjective

When you act wild and noisy, you are being **rambunctious**.

The children were being so **rambunctious** that the librarian asked them to go outside.

Which ones are acting **rambunctious**?

- Grandma and Grandpa going for a quiet walk
- children playing a game of tag
- puppies fighting over a bone
- the audience at a piano recital
- clowns at a circus performance

Tell about a time when you were acting too **rambunctious**. What were you doing? What happened?

A Word a Day, Primary • EMC 2717 • ©2002 by Evan-Moor Corp.

inquire

verb

When you **inquire**, you try to find out something by asking a question.

For information on when the movie begins, you can **inquire** at the ticket window.

Are you **inquiring** when you

- call your grandma to wish her a happy birthday?
- ask a librarian where to find a book?
- call your friend to ask when his party starts?
- ask your mom to check your homework?
- ask someone for directions to a new store?

Do you think it's a good idea to **inquire** when you aren't sure about something? Why or why not?

clench

verb

You **clench** something when you squeeze it tightly.

The baseball player **clenched** the bat as he stepped up to home plate.

Which of these could you **clench**?

- a hammer when you're building a bookcase
- a hot dog at a picnic
- your teeth during a scary movie
- a fragile cup as you drink tea
- your friend's arm on a roller coaster ride

When do you **clench** your teeth? When do you **clench** your fists?

A Word a Day

monotone
noun

When you speak in a **monotone**, you don't use any expression in your voice.

The speaker's **monotone** almost put the audience to sleep.

Which of the following might sound like a **monotone**?

- words spoken by a computer
- a dramatic poem read by its author
- an electronic voice on an answering machine
- a person calling out for help
- someone telling a joke

Say your name, age, favorite color, and favorite food in a **monotone**. Then try it again with lots of expression. Which do you prefer? Why?

nibble
verb

You **nibble** your food when you eat it with small bites.

My pet rat **nibbled** on a piece of cheese for fifteen minutes before he finished it.

Which ones might **nibble**?

- a wolf eating its prey
- a queen eating a tea cake
- a person in a pie-eating contest
- a child tasting a new kind of food
- a bear with a honeycomb

What is your favorite food to **nibble**?

A Word a Day, Primary • EMC 2717 • ©2002 by Evan-Moor Corp.

attire

noun

The clothing you wear, especially for a fancy occasion, is your **attire**.

The proper **attire** for the banquet and ball is a suit or a gown.

Which of these could be part of a bride's **attire**?

- a white gown
- hiking boots
- a baseball cap
- a veil
- high-heeled shoes

The last time you had to dress up for a special occasion, what was your **attire**?

spectator

noun

A **spectator** is a person who watches an event without participating in it.

I usually like to play basketball, but today I'm going to be a **spectator** in the stands.

Which of these is a **spectator**?

- a father at his daughter's soccer game
- the catcher on a baseball team
- a sports reporter at the Olympics
- a runner in a race
- a tennis player on the court

Which sport do you enjoy as a **spectator**? Which sport do you enjoy as a player?

A Word a Day

omit

verb

When you **omit** something, you leave it out.

If you **omit** your name on your book report, your teacher won't know whose it is.

Which one of these is OK to **omit**?

- the day of the week when you write the date
- a letter in a word on a spelling test
- the time of your birthday party on your invitations
- one of the numbers in your telephone number
- your middle name when you write your name on your paper

When you tell your family about your day at school, what information might you **omit**? What information would you share?

brim

noun

The **brim** is the edge of a cup or bowl.

The tea spilled over the **brim** of the cup and into the saucer.

Which of the following could you fill to the **brim**?

- a soup bowl
- a pencil
- a bucket
- a fork
- a coffee mug

If you had to drink a cup of something that was filled to the **brim**, what would it be?

A Word a Day, Primary • EMC 2717 • ©2002 by Evan-Moor Corp.

grumble

verb

When you **grumble**, you complain in a grumpy way.

My brother always **grumbles** when Mom reminds him to do his chores.

Which of these would make you **grumble**?

- having to get up early to take out the garbage
- getting ten dollars from Grandpa for your birthday
- getting invited to the movies
- having to stay in during recess and clean the desks
- forgetting to take your lunch to school

What is something you **grumble** about? What is something you heard someone else **grumble** about?

topple

verb

When something falls down, it **topples**.

The tree was about to **topple** over in the strong wind.

Which things could **topple** easily?

- a large stone statue
- a house
- a child learning to ride a bike
- a tower of building blocks
- a car

How would you stand to keep someone from **toppling** you?

A Word a Day

zany

adjective

A person who acts **zany** behaves in a foolish or silly way.

The **zany** clown was honking a giant horn and squirting water from a flower on his coat.

Which words describe someone who acts **zany**?

- calm
- wacky
- nutty
- serious
- angry

Do you like acting **zany** or being around someone who's acting **zany**? Why or why not?

putrid

adjective

Something **putrid** is rotten and smells awful.

After sitting in the sun for two days, the garbage was **putrid**.

Which of these might smell **putrid**?

- the town dump
- a compost pile
- a flower garden
- spoiled milk
- freshly baked bread

Have you ever smelled something **putrid**? What was it? What did you do?

A Word a Day, Primary • EMC 2717 • ©2002 by Evan-Moor Corp.

echo

noun

A sound that gets softer as it repeats is an **echo**.

After I yelled down to the hikers at the bottom of the canyon, the **echo** of my voice came back: "Hello . . . hello . . . hello . . . "

In which of these places might you hear an **echo**?

- the halls of an empty building
- a mountain overlooking a valley
- a crowded department store
- your bedroom
- a long tunnel

If you were in a place that made a good **echo**, what would you like to say?

infant

noun

An **infant** is a baby.

The **infant** was sleeping peacefully in her crib.

Which words can describe an **infant**?

- tiny
- mighty
- mean
- precious
- noisy

Do you have any pictures of yourself as an **infant**? Tell about one of them.

A Word a Day

ability

noun

An **ability** is a skill or talent that you have.

Jill has the **ability** to hear a song and then play it on the piano.

Which of these take a special **ability**?

- breathing
- singing
- playing a violin
- eating
- winning a chess tournament

What special **ability** do you have? Which would you like to have? Tell about someone you know who has a special **ability**.

dynamo

noun

A **dynamo** is an active person with lots of energy and enthusiasm.

Diana is a **dynamo**, performing in the school show, playing on the soccer team, and running for class president!

Would you be a **dynamo** if you

- slept until noon all summer?
- ran around the track more times than the coach asked you to?
- organized a recycling project at your school?
- moved as slowly as a snail?
- led the cheering section for the football team?

Are you a **dynamo**, or do you know someone who is? What makes you or the person you know a **dynamo**?

trivial

adjective

When something is **trivial**, it has little importance.

Your book report doesn't need to mention the number of illustrations in the story. That's **trivial** information.

Which of the following information about you is **trivial**?

- your name
- the number of times you blinked your eyes today
- your birthday
- the color of your socks
- your phone number

Share some **trivial** information about yourself or your family with the class.

camouflage

noun

When colors and patterns are used to hide people, animals, or things, they give them **camouflage**.

When a chameleon changes color to blend into the environment, it uses **camouflage**.

Which animals use **camouflage**?

- a polar bear in white snow
- a spotted cow in a green pasture
- a green lizard on a green leaf
- a red rooster on a white fence
- a seagull at the beach

If you wanted to use **camouflage** in the woods, what would you wear? Do you think wearing **camouflage** is a good idea? Why?

A Word a Day

hue

noun

A **hue** is a color or a shade of color.

I couldn't decide whether to color the flower a light or dark red **hue**.

"Strawberry red" and "rose red" are the names of **hues**. Choose a descriptive name for each of these **hues**:

- light blue
- dark yellow
- bright orange
- light pink
- medium green

A rainbow has seven colors. Which **hue** is your favorite? What do you own in that **hue**?

wince

verb

You **wince** when you pull back or make a face in fear or pain.

I **wince** every time my pet snake eats a mouse.

Would you **wince** if you

- got an A on a test?
- were getting a shot?
- were having a birthday party?
- had to take bad-tasting medicine?
- got your tooth drilled by the dentist?

Describe a situation that makes you **wince**.

A Word a Day, Primary • EMC 2717 • ©2002 by Evan-Moor Corp.

compromise

verb

You **compromise** when both people give in a little to settle a disagreement.

When Linda wanted to read and Janie wanted to watch a video, they **compromised** by listening to a book on tape.

In which of these situations could people **compromise**?

- You're invited to a beach party on the day of your family reunion.
- Your brother wants macaroni, but you want pizza.
- Your dad gets a $25 traffic ticket, but he only wants to pay $10.
- Half the class wants to play tag, but the others want to play ball.
- Mom wants to go to Hawai'i, but Dad wants to go hiking.

Choose one of the situations listed above and tell how the people might **compromise**.

flimsy

adjective

Something that is weak and lightweight is **flimsy**.

The weight of the books broke the **flimsy** box when I picked it up.

Which of these is **flimsy**?

- a brick
- the bathroom sink
- a piece of tracing paper
- a spider web
- a bronze statue

Find something in the class that is **flimsy**. Find something else that is not. Compare the two things. How are they alike and how are they different?

A Word a Day

jealous

adjective

When you want something that someone else has, you feel **jealous**.

Sarah felt **jealous** when her friend got a bike like the one she wanted.

Would you be **jealous** if your friend

- had a toothache?

- got a scooter?

- won a trip to Hawai'i?

- lost her cat?

- broke an arm?

Tell about a time when you felt **jealous**. What made you feel that way? How does it feel to be **jealous**?

bashful

adjective

Someone who is **bashful** feels shy, especially around new people.

The new student was so **bashful** that she turned red when the teacher introduced her.

In which of these situations might you be **bashful**?

- talking to your dog

- playing with your best friend

- joining a new class at a different school

- meeting the president of the United States

- reciting a poem in front of the whole school

When were you in a situation where you felt **bashful**? What happened?

18

abundant

adjective

Something is **abundant** when you have a lot of it.

The farmer's corn crop was so **abundant** that his grain silo was filled to the top.

Which of the following describe an **abundant** amount?

- a sack of rice
- a kernel of corn
- a hill of ants
- a sheet of paper
- a grain of sand

If you could have an **abundant** supply of something, what would it be?

neglected

verb

When something is **neglected**, it has not been cared for well.

He **neglected** his plants all summer, so they died.

Which of these is OK to **neglect**?

- a pet
- a broken toy
- a paper flower
- your homework
- your friend's feelings

What is something that you've **neglected**? What happened as a result? What is something you haven't **neglected**? Use the list above for ideas.

A Word a Day

grant

verb

When you **grant** something to someone, you allow him or her to have it.

The fairy waved her magic wand and said, "I will **grant** you one wish."

Which of these could someone really **grant**?

- permission to leave class to get a drink of water
- a license to fly a space shuttle
- permission to live 200 years
- a license to fish in a stream or an ocean
- permission to stay up late on the weekend

Imagine that you have been magically transported into a fairy tale. A genie pops out of a lamp and will **grant** you three wishes. What will you wish for and why?

talented

adjective

When you have a natural ability to do something well, you are **talented**.

The **talented** young singer sang as well as a professional recording artist.

Would you need to be **talented** in order to

- tie your shoelaces?
- play in an orchestra?
- paint a picture that was shown in a museum?
- sharpen a pencil?
- juggle three flaming torches?

If you could be **talented** at anything in the world, what would it be? Explain your answer. What are you already **talented** at?

A Word a Day, Primary • EMC 2717 • ©2002 by Evan-Moor Corp.

opinion

noun

Your **opinion** is what you think about something.

I thought the movie would be exciting, but I changed my **opinion** after I saw it.

Which of these is an **opinion**?

- The sun rises in the morning.
- Your teacher is smart.
- People have to eat to stay alive.
- Red is the best color.
- Spelling is fun.

Share your **opinion** about one of these ideas:

Students should be given more homework.

Students should have longer recess breaks.

It's fun to do chores.

pursue

verb

When you **pursue** something, you follow or chase it in an attempt to get it.

She is going to **pursue** her dream of being a doctor no matter how long it takes.

Which of these are examples of **pursuing** something?

- a cat chasing a mouse
- a girl riding a bicycle
- a police officer running after a thief
- a student following his or her teacher's instructions
- a child following a ball that rolled away

What is a dream you want to **pursue** in the future?

A Word a Day

obnoxious

adjective

When something is disagreeable and unpleasant, it is **obnoxious**.

The play was ruined by some **obnoxious** people in the audience who were talking during the show.

Which of the following are examples of **obnoxious** behavior?

- throwing food at your friends during lunch
- sitting quietly and reading a book
- bringing a nice gift to a birthday party
- grabbing a book out of someone's hands
- singing in the library

Have you ever seen someone being **obnoxious**? What was the person doing? How did you feel about it?

abolish

verb

When you **abolish** something, you get rid of it.

I would like to **abolish** pollution.

Which words mean about the same thing as **abolish**?

- continue
- wipe out
- destroy
- save
- keep

If you could choose one thing to **abolish**, what would it be?

A Word a Day, Primary • EMC 2717 • ©2002 by Evan-Moor Corp.

scholar

noun

A **scholar** is a person who has studied and learned a lot.

Professor Rossi, the famous music **scholar**, has studied music all his life.

Which of these would a **scholar** probably do?

- get to class late
- spend time in the library
- play in a rock and roll band
- enjoy reading and writing
- discuss interesting ideas

How are you like a **scholar**? In what ways could you be a better **scholar**?

vigorous

adjective

When something is **vigorous**, it is strong, active, and full of energy.

Vigorous exercise makes your heart work harder.

Which of the following are **vigorous**?

- a weight lifter
- a patient in the hospital
- a firefighter
- a sleeping baby
- a playful puppy

What is your favorite **vigorous** activity? What do you enjoy about it?

A Word a Day

etiquette

noun

The rules of polite behavior, especially for social situations, are called **etiquette**.

It is good **etiquette** to chew with your mouth closed.

Which statements are good rules of **etiquette**?

- Sit up straight at the dinner table.
- Throw any food you don't like on the floor.
- Talk with your mouth full of food.
- Keep your napkin on your lap when you're not using it.
- Remember to say "please" and "thank you."

What are some rules of **etiquette** that you follow?

disturb

verb

You **disturb** someone when you bother, annoy, or interrupt him or her.

I hung a sign on my door that said "Do Not **Disturb**" so that I could study.

Which of these might **disturb** you if you were trying to sleep?

- loud music
- an ambulance siren outside your window
- a leaf falling
- someone snoring loudly across the room
- your dog sleeping in the kitchen

Tell about a time when someone **disturbed** you. What did the person do, and how did you feel?

A Word a Day, Primary • EMC 2717 • ©2002 by Evan-Moor Corp.

miniature

adjective

Something **miniature** is very tiny.

The **miniature** cars in my collection look just like real ones.

Which words describe something that's **miniature**?

- small
- huge
- enormous
- teensy
- little

If you could have a **miniature** toy, what would it be?

bizarre

adjective

Something that's odd or strange in appearance or behavior is **bizarre**.

The alien costume with three eyes and shiny scales was very **bizarre**.

Would it be **bizarre** if

- you woke up and were ten feet tall?
- a rabbit liked to eat carrots?
- your pet rat started talking to you?
- the characters in your favorite cartoon came out of the TV?
- the food in your refrigerator was cold?

What is the most **bizarre** thing you've ever seen or heard about?

A Word a Day

companion

noun

A **companion** keeps someone company.

The guide dog was the blind woman's constant **companion**.

Which of the following are **companions**?

- a baby-sitter and a small child
- a cashier and a customer at a store
- two friends walking together on a beach
- a waiter and a diner at a restaurant
- a pet and its owner

What do you enjoy doing with a **companion**?

trio

noun

A group of three is a **trio**.

The three girls called their singing **trio** "Wee Three."

Which of these circus acts would be introduced as a **trio**?

- two guys and a girl juggling plates
- a unicycle rider
- three ladies riding horses bareback
- two clowns being shot out of a canon
- three dancing bears

What activities have you done with two other friends as a **trio**?

A Word a Day, Primary • EMC 2717 • ©2002 by Evan-Moor Corp.

retrieve

verb

When you get something back again, you **retrieve** it.

I had to **retrieve** my homework from the trash after I threw it away by mistake.

Which of these could you **retrieve**?

- the food you ate for lunch yesterday
- a book that fell down the stairs
- a newspaper in your recycling bin
- a button that went down the drain
- the sunset that you watched last week

What is something that you had to **retrieve**? Where did you **retrieve** it from?

alert

adjective

When you're **alert**, you're wide awake and able to act quickly.

A deer in the forest must be **alert** to protect itself from predators.

Would you be **alert** if

- you fell asleep in class?
- you caught someone who was trying to sneak up behind you?
- you're the first one to follow the directions to solve a puzzle?
- your mom has to ask you the same question three times?
- you see smoke coming out of a neighbor's window and call 911?

When is it a good idea to be **alert**? When is it not so important?

A Word a Day

hodgepodge

noun

A **hodgepodge** is a disorderly jumbled mess.

Jimmy could not find his truck in the **hodgepodge** of toys on his floor.

Which of these is a **hodgepodge**?

- a neat stack of books
- a pile of mismatched shoes
- windblown papers all over the floor
- pillows placed neatly on a bed
- scraps of fabric in a rag bag

Which things are in a **hodgepodge** in your room? Which are kept neat and tidy?

frisky

adjective

Someone or something that is playful and lively is **frisky**.

The **frisky** puppy never seemed to tire of chasing the ball.

Which words describe something that is **frisky**?

- active
- exhausted
- fun-loving
- sleepy
- joyful

Where have you seen a **frisky** animal? What was it doing?

A Word a Day, Primary • EMC 2717 • ©2002 by Evan-Moor Corp.

affection

noun

When you show **affection**, you show feelings of love and caring.

Mai's puppy showed **affection** by licking her face.

Which ones show **affection**?

- getting a hug from your mom
- giving someone a valentine
- stepping on someone's toe
- bringing flowers to your grandmother
- borrowing your brother's favorite shirt without asking

What are things that you do to show **affection**? What are ways **affection** is shown to you?

scarce

adjective

Something is **scarce** if it's hard to find.

Hummingbirds are **scarce** at the South Pole.

Which of these might be **scarce**?

- rivers in the desert
- snow on a mountain in winter
- sand on a beach
- gold coins at the bottom of the ocean
- ants at a picnic

What is something that's **scarce** that you wish you had?

A Word a Day

inhabit

verb

You **inhabit** the place where you live.

Bats have **inhabited** that cave for many years.

Which of these places can people **inhabit**?

- an apartment
- the moon
- a trailer
- a lake
- an island

What are some of the places your family has **inhabited** since you were born?

identical

adjective

When things are exactly alike, they're **identical**.

The twins were so **identical** that you could not tell one from the other.

Which words describe things that are **identical**?

- different
- same
- matching
- unusual
- opposite

Do you own anything that's **identical** to something that someone else owns? What is it?

A Word a Day, Primary • EMC 2717 • ©2002 by Evan-Moor Corp.

participate

verb

When you take part in something, you **participate**.

She didn't want to **participate** in the game, so she just watched.

In which of these can you **participate**?

- a game of dodgeball
- the Olympic Games
- a children's sports team
- a motorcycle race
- a spelling bee

What activities did you **participate** in this week during recess?

braggart

noun

A **braggart** is someone who brags or shows off.

The **braggart** couldn't stop showing off his prize and talking about how great he was.

Which of these would a **braggart** do?

- repeat the story of his success over and over
- put his trophy in a closet
- tell his friends that he's the best at everything
- tell the other team, "I hope you win next time"
- shout, "I won, I won, I won!"

Think about someone who acted like a **braggart**. How did you feel about his or her behavior?

A Word a Day

decay

verb

When something **decays**, it becomes rotten.

If you don't want your teeth to **decay**, you need to brush them regularly.

Which of these could **decay**?

- a leaf
- a glass of water
- a piece of wood
- a slice of bread
- a windowpane

What can cause your teeth to **decay**? What do you do so that your teeth won't **decay**?

modern

adjective

Something that is from recent times is **modern**.

Modern refrigerators use much less energy than older ones.

Which of the following are **modern**?

- a covered wagon
- a space shuttle
- a solar-powered car
- a woodburning stove
- a scooter

What **modern** inventions are a part of your life that did not exist when your parents were children? How would your life be different without some of the **modern** inventions we have now?

A Word a Day, Primary • EMC 2717 • ©2002 by Evan-Moor Corp.

object

verb

You **object** when you express your disagreement with something.

My parents would **object** if a restaurant wouldn't allow children to eat there.

Which of these is a way to **object**?

- "I don't agree with you."
- "You're absolutely right."
- "That is just not appropriate."
- "I like the way you said that."
- "I think you're wrong."

Tell about a time when you said or did something and someone **objected** to it. Now tell about a time when you **objected** to something someone else did or said.

grip

verb

When you hold something very tightly you **grip** it.

The climber **gripped** the rope as she made her way up the steep mountain.

Which words mean about the same thing as **grip**?

- hold on
- clutch
- drop
- grab
- let go

Tell about a time when you would have fallen if you hadn't had something to **grip**. Where were you? What did you **grip**?

A Word a Day

abbreviated

adjective

A word that is written in a shortened form is **abbreviated**.

The **abbreviated** form of Texas is TX.

What is the complete form of each of these **abbreviated** words?

- Mrs.
- Dr.
- St.
- Ave.
- Mr.

Do you have any **abbreviated** words in your address? What are they?

bargain

noun

Something that is bought for a cheap price is a **bargain**.

The flea market is a great place to find lots of **bargains**!

Which of these is probably a **bargain**?

- candy bars for $5 each
- two pairs of pants for the price of one
- buy two pairs of shoes and get one free
- movie tickets for half price before 6:00 p.m.
- two dollars extra to split a main course at a restaurant

Tell about a time when you went shopping and found a real **bargain**. Why does it feel good to get something that's a **bargain**?

A Word a Day, Primary • EMC 2717 • ©2002 by Evan-Moor Corp.

daily

adjective

When something happens **daily**, it happens every day.

My parents read the paper **daily** to keep up with world news.

Which of these happen **daily**?

- your birthday
- the sunrise
- a test at school
- brushing your teeth
- eating

Tell about three things that you do **daily**. Then talk about things that you do not do **daily**. What would it be like if you celebrated your birthday **daily**?

emotion

noun

An **emotion** is a feeling.

Actors express **emotions** from sadness and disappointment to excitement and joy.

Which words name an **emotion**?

- love
- heat
- anger
- fright
- stickiness

What do you do when you feel **emotions** like frustration or anger? How about when you feel excitement or joy? Which **emotions** do you prefer?

A Word a Day

feeble

adjective

Someone or something that is **feeble** is weak or frail.

After recovering from his illness, the **feeble** man had to walk with a cane.

Which of these describe someone or something **feeble**?

- a newly hatched baby bird
- an elderly person in a wheelchair
- a playful puppy
- an injured bunny
- a weight lifter

Have you ever felt **feeble**? What was it like? What can you do to help someone who is **feeble**?

gallant

adjective

A **gallant** person is brave and courteous.

The **gallant** knight rescued the princess from the fire-breathing dragon.

Would a **gallant** person

- throw food in a food fight?
- lead the way through a dark forest?
- hold the door open to let someone through?
- refuse to share with others?
- go into a burning building to save a child?

Tell about a time when you or someone you know did something very **gallant**. What do you think of a person who is **gallant**?

A Word a Day, Primary • EMC 2717 • ©2002 by Evan-Moor Corp.

hardy

adjective

When someone or something is **hardy**, it can survive in difficult conditions.

The **hardy** cactus can survive the blistering desert sun.

Which words are similar in meaning to **hardy**?

- tough
- fragile
- strong
- flimsy
- sturdy

Tell about a person, animal, or plant that you think is **hardy**. What experience did it go through that makes you think it's **hardy**?

gleam

verb

Something that **gleams** shines and gives off or reflects a glow of light.

The medal **gleamed** as it was hung around the winner's neck.

Which of these might **gleam**?

- mud
- diamonds
- the sun
- a newly waxed car
- dirty dishes

What is something you own—or that you would like to own—that **gleams**? How do you keep it **gleaming**?

A Word a Day

harmony

noun

If you work in total cooperation with others, you work in **harmony**.

The ball players worked in such **harmony** that they easily won the game.

Which words mean something similar to **harmony**?

- argument
- agreement
- friendship
- togetherness
- disagreement

Tell about something that you do in **harmony** with your classmates, your family, or a friend. Do you think people are able to get more done when they work in **harmony**?

ideal

adjective

Something that is just perfect is **ideal**.

The timing was **ideal**; the bus arrived just as we got to the bus stop!

Which statements describe something that is really **ideal**?

- Summer is the ideal time to go snowboarding.
- A fish is an ideal pet because it takes very little care.
- The ideal place for that plant is in the garden.
- I think it would be ideal if I lost the race.
- A sunny day is ideal for a baseball game.

Tell about your **ideal** vacation. Where would you go, who would you take, and what would you do there? What would be an **ideal** souvenir to bring home?

A Word a Day, Primary • EMC 2717 • ©2002 by Evan-Moor Corp.

jovial

adjective

A **jovial** person is always laughing and in a good mood.

Our **jovial** neighbor always has a funny joke or silly trick for us.

Which of these describe a **jovial** person?

- jolly
- angry
- fun-loving
- mean
- cheerful

Tell about someone you know who is **jovial**. What makes him or her a **jovial** person? What is fun about being around that person?

loaf

verb

You **loaf** when you spend time lounging around doing nothing.

I would rather **loaf** on the weekend than do my chores and yard work.

Which of the following are examples of someone who likes to **loaf**?

- fixing the sink yourself instead of calling the plumber
- taking a nap outside in a hammock
- sitting in the sun and reading
- working all afternoon in the garden
- spending several hours doing homework

What do you like to do when you **loaf**? Do you prefer **loafing** or being active?

A Word a Day

milestone

noun

A **milestone** is an event of major importance.

The baby's first birthday was a **milestone** that was celebrated with a big party.

Which of these would be a **milestone**?

- taking a bath
- the first day of kindergarten
- going to the grocery store
- graduating from high school
- winning a war of independence

Tell about a **milestone** in your life. It could be the first time you learned to ride a bike or having a new brother or sister. How did this **milestone** affect your life?

nominate

verb

You **nominate** someone when you suggest that he or she would be good for a job or for special recognition.

I want to **nominate** Henry for class president because he has lots of good ideas.

Which statements might somebody make when they **nominate** a person?

- "I think April should do the dishes tonight."
- "Gabe would be the best carnival clown."
- "Don't choose Ricky because he's always late."
- "Brittany should get the award for best reader."
- "Diego doesn't want to be team captain."

Who would you **nominate** for the award of "Most Helpful Person in the School?"

A Word a Day, Primary • EMC 2717 • ©2002 by Evan-Moor Corp.

occupy

verb

You **occupy** a place when you live in it or use it.

We can **occupy** the house just as soon as they finish painting it.

Which of these could an animal **occupy**?

- a seashell
- a cave
- an umbrella
- a tree
- a trumpet

If you could **occupy** any sort of building for your home, what would you choose?

persevere

verb

You **persevere** when you keep trying and don't give up even if it's difficult.

The hikers felt like giving up after an hour, but they **persevered** and made it to the top of the mountain.

Which of these would you say if you plan to **persevere**?

- "Forget it; it's too hard."
- "I know I can do it!"
- "I can't go any farther."
- "I'll never give up no matter how long it takes me."
- "I'll do it over and over until I get it right."

Tell about a time when you or someone you know thought something was really hard and almost gave up, but **persevered**. How did it feel?

A Word a Day

queasy

adjective

If you feel sick to your stomach or nauseated, you feel **queasy**.

The rolling of the boat during the storm made everyone feel **queasy**.

Which of these might make a person feel **queasy**?

- eating too much candy
- riding a roller coaster
- sitting quietly in a chair
- eating food that's too spicy
- going for a walk

Tell about a time when someone you know felt **queasy**. What did he or she do to feel better? What are some things that make you feel **queasy**?

racket

noun

A **racket** is a lot of very loud noise.

The talking birds in the pet store made an awful **racket**.

Which of these would make a **racket**?

- a dripping faucet
- children yelling at a ball game
- ambulance sirens
- a goldfish swimming in a bowl
- dogs barking at a cat

In what kind of place is it all right to make a **racket**? Where isn't it OK?

A Word a Day, Primary • EMC 2717 • ©2002 by Evan-Moor Corp.

secluded

adjective

A **secluded** place is quiet and out of sight.

The pirates hid the treasure on the most **secluded** part of the island.

Which of these places is **secluded**?

- a city bus stop
- a house on a lonely hilltop
- a cabin in the woods
- a grocery store
- an airport

If you could create your own **secluded** place, where would it be and what would you have in it? What can you do to have quiet, **secluded** time to yourself even in your own house?

tedious

adjective

If something is boring and repetitious, it's **tedious**.

We thought it was **tedious** to write all of our spelling words ten times.

Which words mean about the same thing as **tedious**?

- exciting
- fun
- boring
- dull
- tiresome

What is something you have to do that you think is **tedious**?

A Word a Day

advertise

verb

You **advertise** when you give information to the public or announce that something is for sale.

My dad had to **advertise** in the paper for a week before he sold our old car.

Which of the following might be **advertised**?

- a sale at a department store
- puppies for sale
- the time you go to bed
- a job at a restaurant
- your favorite flavor of ice cream

How would you **advertise** a bicycle that you had for sale?

convince

verb

You **convince** someone when you make him or her think about something the way that you do.

I couldn't **convince** my mother to let me stay up late on a school night.

Which of these are examples of a person trying to **convince** someone?

- telling a teacher that your work will be better if you have another day to finish it
- asking a friend what her favorite color is
- telling your parents why you should be able to sleep over at a friend's house
- asking your sister to leave your room
- telling your parents why you need a bigger allowance

Tell about a time when you **convinced** your parents to change their minds about something.

A Word a Day, Primary • EMC 2717 • ©2002 by Evan-Moor Corp.

diminish

verb

Something can **diminish** when it is made smaller.

The hunk of cheese **diminished** as the mouse nibbled at it.

Which of the following can **diminish** in size?

- an ice-cream cone as you eat it
- a lollipop as you lick it
- a light bulb when it's left on
- a balloon with a pinhole in it
- a chair as you sit on it

If you could have something that would never **diminish**, what would it be?

interview

verb

You **interview** someone when you meet and ask questions in order to publish the information or broadcast it on radio or television.

The sports reporter was eager to **interview** the players on the winning team.

Which of these might you do during an **interview**?

- laugh
- write a poem
- write notes
- take a short nap
- use a tape recorder

If you could **interview** anybody, who would it be? What would you ask?

A Word a Day

hideous

adjective

Something **hideous** is ugly or horrible to look at.

The monster in the movie was so **hideous**, I had to close my eyes.

Which of these might be **hideous**?

- a rotting jack-o'-lantern
- a rainbow
- a beautiful red rose
- a pack of wolves devouring a deer
- a vampire mask

What is something **hideous** that you've seen? How did you react?

tremble

verb

When you shake with fear, excitement, or cold, you **tremble**.

I was so nervous before the race that I started to **tremble**.

In which of these situations might you **tremble**?

- riding the scariest roller coaster at the amusement park
- walking through a snowstorm without a jacket
- writing your name on your homework paper
- talking to your friend on the phone
- going on stage to accept an award

Tell about a time when you **trembled** from fear. Now tell about a time when you **trembled** from the cold. What is the difference in feelings, and which do you prefer?

A Word a Day, Primary • EMC 2717 • ©2002 by Evan-Moor Corp.

volume

noun

The loudness of a sound or noise is its **volume**.

We always turn down the **volume** on the TV when someone is on the phone.

Which of these has a **volume** control?

- a lamp
- a TV/VCR
- a CD player
- a shoe
- a tape recorder

What were you doing the last time someone asked you to turn down the **volume**?

famous

adjective

A **famous** person is known or recognized by many people.

Everyone wanted to see the **famous** star who was in town to make a movie.

Which of the following people are **famous**?

- a member of a popular rock and roll band
- the cashier at the supermarket
- the president of the United States
- your mailman
- George Washington

What would you like to be **famous** for?

A Word a Day

complicated

adjective

If something is **complicated**, it's difficult to understand.

My dad helped me follow the **complicated** directions for building my model car.

Which of these would probably be **complicated**?

- writing your full name
- a college math book
- flossing your teeth
- the plans for a skyscraper
- writing instructions for building a greenhouse

What is something **complicated** that you've tried to do? How did it turn out?

predict

verb

You **predict** the future when you say what you think is going to happen.

Weather forecasters use computers to help **predict** the weather.

Which sentences **predict** something?

- I think I'm going to get an A on my test tomorrow.
- I had scrambled eggs for breakfast yesterday.
- I can guess what this book is about from the picture and title on the cover.
- I woke up late for school and missed the bus.
- "I bet it's the mailman," said Mom when she heard a knock at the door.

Try to **predict** what you'll have for dinner tonight. Tomorrow you can report on whether you **predicted** correctly.

A Word a Day, Primary • EMC 2717 • ©2002 by Evan-Moor Corp.

shipshape

adjective

If something is clean, neat, and in order, it's **shipshape**.

We don't get our weekly allowance until our room is **shipshape**.

Which of the following are **shipshape**?

- a library with books neatly organized on shelves
- toys stored nicely in a toy box
- a room with laundry thrown all over the floor
- the cafeteria after a food fight
- clothes hung neatly in a closet

How do you help keep your classroom **shipshape**? How about your room at home?

agony

noun

If you're in **agony**, you're experiencing very strong pain.

I was in **agony** when I fell and broke my arm.

Would you be in **agony** if

- you were taking a bubble bath?
- a brick fell on your bare foot?
- you were eating an ice-cream cone?
- you got a terrible sunburn?
- you had an awful toothache?

Tell about a time when you were in **agony**. What did you do to feel better?

A Word a Day

chitchat

verb

When you **chitchat**, you talk about unimportant things.

My mom likes to **chitchat** on the phone with her sister about how her day went.

Which topics might you **chitchat** about?

- today's weather
- a family member's major surgery
- the color of a new nail polish
- your neighbor's serious car accident
- your brother's new haircut

What do you like to **chitchat** about with your friends?

occupation

noun

An **occupation** is a person's job or career.

A firefighter has an exciting and dangerous **occupation**.

Which **occupations** are performed outdoors?

- gardening
- farming
- teaching
- writing
- collecting garbage

What **occupation** would you like to have someday? Why are you interested in it?

A Word a Day, Primary • EMC 2717 • ©2002 by Evan-Moor Corp.

wealthy

adjective

Someone who has a lot of money or property is **wealthy**.

Our **wealthy** neighbors own three cars, two boats, and a beach house.

Which ones are probably **wealthy**?

- a family who owns an airplane
- someone who doesn't own any shoes
- a person who lives in a mansion
- someone who shops at the flea market
- somebody who wins the lottery prize

What would you do to help others if you were **wealthy**?

consent

noun

Consent is permission to do something.

My parents have to give their written **consent** for me to go on a class field trip.

Would you need your parents' **consent** to

- spend the night at a friend's house?
- buy ice cream from the ice-cream truck?
- get a drink of water?
- wash your hands?
- stay up later than usual?

What did you ask for the last time you asked your parents for their **consent**? What did they say?

A Word a Day

famished

verb

If you're **famished**, you suffer from extreme hunger.

After I skipped lunch, I was so **famished** that I ate three helpings of everything for dinner.

Would you be **famished** if

- you ate two peas?
- you ate three helpings of mashed potatoes and gravy?
- you hadn't eaten breakfast or lunch?
- you had a big dinner at a restaurant?
- you had the flu and nothing tasted good to you?

Have you ever felt **famished**? Tell about it and how you felt when you finally ate.

hustle

verb

If you **hustle**, you move very quickly and with lots of energy.

We really have to **hustle** if we want to catch the movie that starts in ten minutes.

Which words describe the way you move when you **hustle**?

- like a snail
- as quick as a wink
- sleepily
- like molasses
- like lightning

Tell about a time when you had to **hustle**. What were you doing?

A Word a Day, Primary • EMC 2717 • ©2002 by Evan-Moor Corp.

villain

noun

The **villain** is an evil or wicked character in a story, movie, or play.

In old cowboy movies, the **villain** usually wears black and the hero wears white.

Which of these is something a **villain** would do?

- take soup to a sick friend
- lie about something
- help a hurt puppy
- rob a bank
- try to trick somebody

Can you think of a **villain** in a story you have read or heard? What was the **villain** like?

dependable

adjective

Something or someone you can count on is **dependable**.

The guide dog was a **dependable** helper for the blind teenager.

Which of the following show **dependable** behavior?

- doing the dishes after being asked only once
- always coming right home after baseball practice
- waking up late for school every day
- forgetting to bring homework home from school
- calling to let your parents know if you're going to be late

What are some things you do that show that you are a **dependable** person? What's one thing you could do to become more **dependable**?

A Word a Day

journey

noun

A **journey** is a long trip or an adventure.

The **journey** across the Great Plains took a long time in covered wagons.

Which of these is a **journey**?

- a trip around the corner to the grocery store
- a drive across the United States to see Grandma
- walking next door to play with the neighbor
- traveling across the ocean on a ship
- flying to see your cousin who lives in another country

Have you ever gone on a **journey**? Where did you go? Where would you like to go if you could go on a **journey** anywhere?

attempt

verb

If you **attempt** something, you try to do it.

The juggler was going to **attempt** to juggle six flaming torches.

Which words mean about the same thing as **attempt**?

- try
- fail
- give up
- make an effort
- give it a go

What did you **attempt** that was difficult? What happened?

A Word a Day, Primary • EMC 2717 • ©2002 by Evan-Moor Corp.

forbid

verb

When you **forbid** something, you tell someone they cannot do it.

Most parents **forbid** their children to eat sweets right before dinner.

If you wanted to **forbid** something, which words would you say?

- "Absolutely not!"
- "By all means."
- "Certainly."
- "No way!"
- "Go right ahead."

Do your parents ever **forbid** you from doing something you want to do? Why?

portion

noun

A **portion** is a piece or a part of something.

I only ate one piece of pie, but my brother had a second **portion**.

Which of these is a **portion**?

- a slice of cake
- a dozen eggs
- a chapter of a book
- an order of french fries
- a bag of sugar

What do you like a large **portion** of? What do you want only a small **portion** of?

A Word a Day

vacant

adjective

When a place is empty, it is **vacant**.

The **vacant** house will be painted before other people move in.

Which of these is **vacant**?

- your house
- a hotel room that no one is using
- a store full of customers
- an empty lot
- an apartment with no one living in it

What does it feel like inside a **vacant** house? Compare how it feels to be in a house where a family lives.

huddle

verb

When a group of people or animals crowd together, they **huddle**.

The family tried to **huddle** under an umbrella when they were caught in the rain.

In which of these situations might people **huddle**?

- to keep warm in a snowstorm
- to read a book alone
- to make room for another person in a crowded elevator
- to discuss a secret play during a football game
- to fly a kite on the beach

How does it make you feel to see a group of classmates **huddled** together whispering? Why do you feel like that?

A Word a Day, Primary • EMC 2717 • ©2002 by Evan-Moor Corp.

dismal

adjective

Something **dismal** is dark and gloomy.

Our day at the beach turned **dismal** after the fog rolled in.

Which of these is **dismal**?

- rough seas under a stormy sky
- a picnic on a sunny, cloudless day
- a dark house on Halloween night
- an unlit underground tunnel
- a hot day at a carnival

What can you do to cheer up someone who is feeling **dismal**?

ceremony

noun

A **ceremony** is a service or act held to mark a special occasion.

The graduation **ceremony** was held on the lawn outside the school.

Which of these is observed with a **ceremony**?

- a wedding
- a bedtime story
- Grandma and Grandpa's 50th wedding anniversary
- receiving a gold medal at the Olympic Games
- answering the phone

Tell about a **ceremony** you've attended. What occasion was being celebrated?

A Word a Day

definite

adjective

Something that is **definite** is certain.

My sister was **definite** about going to the movies, but I hadn't made up my mind.

Which of these is a **definite** answer?

- "Yes, let's go right now!"
- "Buy me a ticket for Saturday."
- "I'm not sure; I'll call you back."
- "I'll be there at 3:00 sharp."
- "I'm not sure if I like that; let me take another look."

What is something you feel **definite** about?

abandon

verb

When you **abandon** something, you leave it or give it up forever.

The puppy was so darling that we couldn't imagine why anyone would **abandon** it.

Which words mean about the same thing as **abandon**?

- throw out
- hang on to
- get rid of
- keep
- dump

Tell about something you had to **abandon** (a toy, a project, a house) and how you felt about it.

A Word a Day, Primary • EMC 2717 • ©2002 by Evan-Moor Corp.

combine

verb

You **combine** things when you put two or more together.

You **combine** sugar, flour, butter, and eggs to make cookie dough.

What color do you get when you **combine** each of these colors?

- red and blue
- black and white
- yellow and blue
- red and white
- red and yellow

What do you like to **combine** to make an ice-cream sundae?

harmless

adjective

Something is **harmless** if it's safe and causes no harm or injury.

We thought the snake was poisonous, but it turned out to be **harmless**.

Which of the following activities are **harmless**?

- brushing your hair
- jogging on the freeway
- talking to a friend on the phone
- putting on your pajamas
- being shot out of a cannon at the circus

Tell about something you like to do that's **harmless**. Why is it a good idea to participate in **harmless** activities?

A Word a Day

habit

noun

A **habit** is the usual way you act or do things.

Doing your homework at the same time every day is a good **habit** to get into!

Which of these is a good **habit**?

- eating sweets before going to bed
- looking both ways before crossing the street
- getting to school late every day
- saying "please" and "thank you"
- making your bed every morning

What is one good **habit** you have at home? What is a bad **habit** that you'd like to change?

warning

noun

A **warning** is a message that alerts you to danger.

The fire alarm gives us a loud **warning** to leave the building.

Which of the following are **warnings**?

- "Be careful crossing the street."
- "Hey, we're both reading the same book!"
- "Watch out for that skateboarder!"
- "Don't step in that puddle!"
- "There's a good TV show on tonight."

What **warning** do you often hear at home? What about at school?

A Word a Day, Primary • EMC 2717 • ©2002 by Evan-Moor Corp.

exchange

verb

When you **exchange**, you give something to someone and he or she also gives something to you.

We have a gift **exchange** in our class before the winter holidays.

Which of the following are examples of an **exchange**?

- Ying Mei and Jen gave each other birthday gifts.
- My cousin gave me a new toy.
- My mom took back the broken lamp and got another one.
- Let's trade phone numbers.
- You can't wear my new sweater.

If you could **exchange** something you own for something different, what would it be?

contagious

adjective

Something easily passed or spread to another person is **contagious**.

You're supposed to stay home from school if you have something **contagious**, like chicken pox.

Which of the following are **contagious**?

- measles
- a bad cold
- your hair color
- mumps
- freckles

Some people say that laughter is **contagious**. What does that mean? Do you think it's true?

A Word a Day

artificial

adjective

Something **artificial** is not real or natural.

Dorthea's **artificial** nails looked real, but we knew they weren't.

Which of the following are **artificial**?

- a silver wig
- a sweater made of 100% wool
- an imitation leather couch
- fresh vegetables from the garden
- plastic flowers

Do you think it's better to play football or soccer on **artificial** grass or on real grass? Why?

errand

noun

An **errand** is a short trip to deliver or pick up something.

I went with my mom on her **errands** to the store, the library, and the gas station.

Which of the following are **errands**?

- dropping off a roll of film at the drugstore
- having a picnic in the park
- getting an oil change for the car
- buying groceries at the supermarket
- spending a relaxing day at the swimming pool

What's the last **errand** you went on with someone? Do you like going on **errands**? Why or why not?

A Word a Day, Primary • EMC 2717 • ©2002 by Evan-Moor Corp.

furious

adjective

If you are **furious**, you're extremely angry.

My mom was **furious** when our dog dug up her best rose bush.

Which of these might make someone **furious**?

- winning a prize
- having a wallet stolen
- getting a birthday present
- spilling red paint on a white carpet
- getting a new car

Tell about a time when you were **furious** or when someone was **furious** with you.

doodle

verb

When you **doodle**, you draw or scribble while thinking about something else.

I like to **doodle** squiggly lines on bright paper when I'm listening to music.

Which of these is a **doodle**?

- a happy face
- a painting of mountains, trees, and a rainbow
- a zigzag design
- a drawing of you and your family
- a heart with an arrow through it

Do you **doodle**? If so, when? When you **doodle**, what do you make?

A Word a Day

variety
noun

There is **variety** when you can choose from many different items.

My mom buys a package with a **variety** of small cereal boxes so I can eat a different cereal every day.

Which of these has **variety**?

- a case of grape juice
- a box of 64 different colored crayons
- a package of white paper
- a bag of mixed nuts
- an ice-cream parlor with over 30 flavors of ice cream

Do you like just one flavor of jelly beans, or do you prefer a **variety**?

enormous
adjective

If something is **enormous**, it's extremely large.

I thought a bear was big, but the dinosaur at the museum was **enormous**!

Which of the following could be described as **enormous**?

- a skyscraper
- an elephant
- a spider
- a whale
- a peanut

What is the most **enormous** thing you've ever seen? Describe it.

A Word a Day, Primary • EMC 2717 • ©2002 by Evan-Moor Corp.

shriek

verb

When you **shriek**, you let out a loud piercing scream.

When my mom saw that mouse, she let out a **shriek** that even scared me!

Which of these might make a person **shriek**?

- riding the world's fastest roller coaster
- painting a pretty picture
- stepping barefoot on a slug
- reading a book
- getting hit from behind with a snowball

Tell about a time when you heard someone **shriek**, or when you let out a **shriek**.

pastry

noun

Baked goods made from dough are called **pastry**.

The bakery smelled delicious early in the morning after the **pastry** was baked.

Which of these would you find in the **pastry** section of a supermarket?

- apple pie
- hamburger and french fries
- cinnamon roll
- strawberry tart
- salad

What's your favorite **pastry**? Do you buy it at a store or bakery, or make it at home?

A Word a Day

recite

verb

If you **recite** something, you say it aloud from memory.

Our class learned a poem by heart to **recite** at the school assembly.

Which ones might you learn to **recite**?

- the alphabet
- a page from the phone book
- the words to a song
- a nursery rhyme
- the words in a dictionary

What rhyme or song can you **recite**? **Recite** it to a partner or to the class.

antics

noun

Antics are funny or silly actions.

We loved the clowns' **antics** when they squirted water at each other.

Which of the following are **antics**?

- Mom sewing a Halloween costume
- a puppy chasing its tail
- Grandpa taking a nap in his chair
- monkeys chasing each other through a tree
- children having a pillow fight at a slumber party

What are some of the **antics** you enjoy with your friends?

A Word a Day, Primary • EMC 2717 • ©2002 by Evan-Moor Corp.

essential

adjective

If something is **essential**, it's absolutely necessary.

Chocolate is one of the **essential** ingredients for making brownies.

Which of the following are **essential** for you?

- breathing
- eating
- playing the trombone
- sleeping
- watching television

What is something **essential** that you do every day? Why is it **essential**?

imitate

verb

You **imitate** when you copy something or someone.

Grace tried to **imitate** her sister by dressing like her.

Are you **imitating** if you

- tie your shoelaces in a double knot?
- make your voice sound like a cartoon character?
- write your name on your homework?
- make the same gestures as your teacher when you sing in class?
- get a haircut just like your best friend's?

What animal can you **imitate**? Share your **imitation** with the class.

A Word a Day

lagoon

noun

A **lagoon** is a pond or small area of water near a larger body of water.

Water from the ocean reached the **lagoon** at high tide.

Which of these might you find in a **lagoon**?

- lily pads
- fish
- cars
- ducks
- surfers

Would you feel more comfortable swimming in a **lagoon** or in the ocean? Why?

original

adjective

Something is **original** if it is the first of its kind.

The inventor became famous for all his **original** ideas.

Which of these would be **original**?

- a glass of water
- a new dish made by mixing together several ingredients
- greeting cards with designs created by you
- a poem you wrote for your dad's birthday
- the glass slipper that Cinderella wore to the ball

Tell about an **original** idea you have had (for a game, a drawing, something you wrote). What made it **original**?

A Word a Day, Primary • EMC 2717 • ©2002 by Evan-Moor Corp.

prevent

verb

If you do not allow something to happen, you **prevent** it.

We can **prevent** some diseases by giving vaccinations.

Which of the following can people **prevent**?

- a thunderstorm
- forest fires
- illness
- growth
- the sunrise

Tell about something your parents or teacher **prevented** you from doing. What were their reasons? How did you feel?

available

adjective

If something is ready to be offered or used, it is **available**.

My mom asked Jenny if she was **available** to baby-sit on Friday night.

Which of the following let you know that something is **available**?

- "The doctor can see you now."
- "The tacos you ordered are ready."
- "We won't have that book in the store until next week."
- "I'm sorry; we don't have that sweater in your size right now."
- "There are still a dozen tickets on sale for next week's concert."

Tell about a time you wanted something but it wasn't **available**. What did you do?

A Word a Day

estimate

verb

When you **estimate**, you make a rough or close guess.

There are too many jelly beans to count; let's just **estimate** the number.

Which of these might you need to **estimate**?

- the number of eggs in a dozen
- the amount of water needed by a plant
- the number of people in your family
- the number of people born each day on Earth
- the number of tomatoes needed to make a quart of salsa

How could you make a good **estimate** of the number of people in your school?

cozy

adjective

Something that feels warm, comfortable, and snug is **cozy**.

My **cozy** slippers keep my feet warm on cold winter nights.

Which of these is **cozy**?

- a quilt
- a sweater that makes you itch
- a purring kitten curled in your lap
- flannel pajamas on a chilly night
- a bathing suit

What are your favorite things to help you feel **cozy**?

A Word a Day, Primary • EMC 2717 • ©2002 by Evan-Moor Corp.

clumsy

adjective

Someone or something that moves in an awkward way is **clumsy**.

I felt so **clumsy** when I tripped over my shoelace and dropped my lunch tray.

Would you feel **clumsy** if you

- spilled your glass of juice?
- tripped over the curb and fell?
- won the talent show for dancing?
- could walk on a high wire without falling?
- stepped on your dance partner's toes?

Tell about a time you did something that made you feel **clumsy**. What did you do?

shelter

noun

A **shelter** is a safe place to stay.

When it started pouring, we had to find **shelter** to keep dry.

Which of these could be a **shelter**?

- a cave
- a playground
- a park
- a tree house
- a barn

If you were lost in the woods, what could you use to make a **shelter** for spending the night?

A Word a Day

donate
verb

You **donate** when you give your time, money, or things as a gift to help others.

We will **donate** the money we earn at the fair to help feed homeless children.

Which words mean about the same thing as **donate**?

- offer
- keep
- share
- protect
- contribute

What is something you own that you could **donate** to help a person in need?

swarm
noun

A **swarm** is a large number of insects, animals, or people that move together as a group.

We had to stay inside because a **swarm** of angry bees had just left their hive.

Which of these is a **swarm**?

- a duck in a pond
- a group of people following a parade
- a child playing in the park
- an army of ants moving through the rainforest
- a mass of mosquitoes buzzing around a campground

Have you ever seen or been around a **swarm** of people or insects? Describe what it was like.

A Word a Day, Primary • EMC 2717 • ©2002 by Evan-Moor Corp.

unanimous

adjective

When a decision is **unanimous**, everyone agrees with it.

Everyone in the class voted to go to the zoo, so the **unanimous** decision was approved by the teacher.

Which of the following are examples of **unanimous** decisions?

- Everyone except Henry wanted to go.
- Talia won the election by a 10 to 0 vote.
- The entire school voted to have a carnival.
- The whole team wanted to practice for another hour.
- Jim went to the beach, but Marisela and I stayed home.

Think about a time you participated in making a **unanimous** decision. What was being decided? Was it easy to get everyone to agree?

tempting

adjective

Something that's inviting and hard to resist is **tempting**.

Although I had work to do, his offer to go to the beach was too **tempting** to pass up.

Which of these might be **tempting**?

- getting stung by a bee
- being offered a piece of chocolate cake
- falling out of a tree and breaking your arm
- having your brother or sister offer to do your chores for you
- being invited to go to a concert of your favorite type of music

Tell about a time when something was so **tempting** that you couldn't pass it up.

A Word a Day

accomplishment

noun

An **accomplishment** is something that has been done with success.

It was a major **accomplishment** for the blind hiker to reach the top of the peak.

Which of these is an **accomplishment**?

- learning a difficult piece on the piano
- sitting on the couch watching television
- getting all the words right on a spelling test
- getting a gold medal for winning an Olympic event
- giving up on a math problem after trying to do it once

What is one of your greatest **accomplishments** so far? What other **accomplishments** would you like to achieve in your life?

jiffy

noun

A **jiffy** is a very short amount of time.

She had to tie her shoes in a **jiffy** because she was already late for school.

Which of these could you do in a **jiffy**?

- clap your hands
- zip up your jacket
- turn on a light switch
- make and decorate a cake
- read a book with ten chapters

What do you do to get ready for school that takes only a **jiffy**? What takes longer than a **jiffy**?

A Word a Day, Primary • EMC 2717 • ©2002 by Evan-Moor Corp.

strenuous

adjective

If an activity is **strenuous**, it takes a lot of strength and energy.

After his **strenuous** exercise, the athlete needed to relax and drink some water.

Which of these activities would be **strenuous**?

- moving boxes of heavy books
- picking up a pencil
- doing 100 sit-ups and push-ups
- jumping rope for 20 minutes without stopping
- opening a letter

Tell about a time you did something **strenuous**. How did you feel? What did you do to rest afterwards?

giggle

verb

When you **giggle**, you laugh in a silly or nervous way.

The girls at the slumber party **giggled** as they put makeup on each other.

Which words mean about the same thing as **giggle**?

- chuckle
- shout
- crack up
- weep
- yell

Have you ever had a time when you started to **giggle** and couldn't stop? Where were you and what happened?

A Word a Day

entire

adjective

The **entire** amount is all of it.

It's not a very good idea to eat an **entire** carton of ice cream for dessert.

Which of the following mean about the same thing as **entire**?

- all
- half
- none
- whole
- 100 percent

Is it healthy to eat an **entire** pizza? Why?

consequence

noun

A **consequence** is what happens as the result of another action.

One **consequence** for not doing homework might be getting a poor grade.

What would be the **consequence** for

- leaving your bike out in the rain?
- not returning a library book on time?
- not getting enough sleep at night?
- leaving crayons out in the sun?
- leaving a cake in the oven too long?

Tell about a time you did something and there was a **consequence**. What did you learn?

A Word a Day, Primary • EMC 2717 • ©2002 by Evan-Moor Corp.

humorous

adjective

Something funny or amusing is **humorous**.

The cartoon he brought in was so **humorous** that we all laughed.

Which of these is **humorous**?

- a joke
- a cartoon
- a magician
- a scary movie
- a comic book

Tell about something **humorous** that you have seen or read. What was **humorous** about it?

sturdy

adjective

Something **sturdy** is strong and solid.

The **sturdy** bookshelf was able to hold the weight of many books.

Which of these is **sturdy**?

- a piano
- a large desk
- a feather
- a dish towel
- a refrigerator

What is something in your house that's **sturdy**? How is this useful?

A Word a Day

slither

verb

When you **slither**, you move with a sliding motion.

We watched the snake **slither** up and over the rock on its belly.

Which of the following might **slither**?

- an eel
- a bird
- a snail
- a worm
- a rabbit

Tell about an insect or reptile that you've seen **slither**. How is this way of moving different from the way other animals move?

physician

noun

A **physician** is a doctor.

The **physician** checked my throat, then wrote a prescription for some medicine.

Which of these might a **physician** use?

- a guitar
- a stethoscope
- a thermometer
- a basketball
- an X ray

Tell about a time when you went to a **physician**. Why did you go and what did he or she do?

A Word a Day, Primary • EMC 2717 • ©2002 by Evan-Moor Corp.

assist

verb

When you help someone, you **assist** him or her.

The magician called a volunteer from the audience to **assist** him with a trick.

Which of the following are offers to **assist** someone?

- "I can tie my shoes all by myself!"
- "Let me help you carry the groceries."
- "I built this model airplane without any help!"
- "I'll come over and help you paint the room."
- "May I show you another way to do this math problem?"

Tell about a time when someone **assisted** you with a problem or you **assisted** someone.

enthusiastic

adjective

If you're really excited about something, you're **enthusiastic** about it.

The children were so **enthusiastic** about going on a vacation that they packed their suitcases a week early!

Would you be **enthusiastic** about

- having a cold?
- winning a contest?
- getting a new puppy?
- going to dinner at your favorite restaurant?
- having a friend spend the night at your house?

Tell about a time when you were really **enthusiastic** about something. How did you feel? Why did you feel that way?

A Word a Day

beverage
noun

A **beverage** is something to drink.

The Hawaiian restaurant was famous for its fruit **beverages**.

Which of the following are **beverages**?

- tea
- milk
- pudding
- potato chips
- hot chocolate

Name a **beverage** you have at each meal. What is your favorite **beverage**?

tidy
adjective

A **tidy** place is very neat with everything in order.

Her room was so **tidy** that she could always find anything she needed.

Which of these mean about the same thing as **tidy**?

- clean
- sloppy
- orderly
- messy
- organized

Do you like your room to be **tidy**? Why or why not? What do you do to keep your room **tidy**?

A Word a Day, Primary • EMC 2717 • ©2002 by Evan-Moor Corp.

detour

noun

A **detour** is a route you can follow when the main route is closed for some reason.

When the street was being paved, we had to take a **detour** to get to our house.

Which of these situations would require a **detour** to be set up?

- The highway is open for travel.
- There will be a street fair downtown.
- There are stoplights at the intersection.
- The freeway ramp is closed due to an accident.
- A parade is planned down the main street in town.

Tell about a time when you had to take a **detour**. Did you get anxious or confused?

perishable

adjective

Something that can spoil or rot is **perishable**.

Because meat is **perishable**, we keep it in the cooler when we go camping.

Which of the following are **perishable**?

- fruit
- milk
- chicken
- shampoo
- a box of cereal

What **perishable** foods do you bring in your lunch? How can you keep **perishable** foods fresh until you eat them?

A Word a Day

impatient

adjective

An **impatient** person is always in a hurry and finds it hard to wait.

The **impatient** man left the bank because the line was too long.

Which of these show **impatient** behavior?

- a toddler screaming for the toy that fell out of her stroller
- a teenager waiting politely until everyone finishes dinner
- a child waiting quietly in line to buy ice cream in a crowded store
- a girl calling for help while the teacher is with someone else
- a boy pulling on his mother's sleeve while she's on the phone

What makes you **impatient**? What can you do so it's not so hard to wait?

appliance

noun

An **appliance** is a household machine that is used for a special purpose.

Our toaster is the oldest **appliance** in our kitchen; the microwave is the newest.

Which of these is a household **appliance**?

- a pillow
- a blender
- a doorknob
- a refrigerator
- a vacuum cleaner

Which **appliance** do you use most often at home? What do you use it for?

A Word a Day, Primary • EMC 2717 • ©2002 by Evan-Moor Corp.

appropriate

adjective

When something is **appropriate**, it is right for that situation.

It's **appropriate** to wear nice clothing to a wedding.

Which of the following activities are **appropriate**?

- throwing food on the floor
- saying "thank you" after receiving a gift
- taking your friend's toy without asking
- wearing a bathing suit to the swimming pool
- raising your hand in school when you have a question

What is the **appropriate** way to behave at an orchestra concert? How about at a rock concert?

mumble

verb

When you **mumble**, you don't speak clearly.

After the dentist numbed her mouth, Ariana couldn't help but **mumble**.

Which words mean about the same thing as **mumble**?

- yell
- mutter
- declare
- murmur
- grumble

What would you say to someone who **mumbles** in order to get him or her to speak more clearly?

A Word a Day

prepare

verb

You **prepare** when you get ready for something.

I studied my math problems to **prepare** for the test.

Which of these show that you have **prepared**?

- You don't know where your homework is.
- You know how to call 911 in an emergency.
- You learn your spelling words before the test.
- You choose your clothes for school the night before.
- You haven't learned your address or phone number yet.

How do you **prepare** for school the night before so that you're ready to go in the morning?

drought

noun

A **drought** is an unusually long period of dry weather.

After months of **drought**, all the crops died.

Which of these can you expect during a **drought**?

- floods
- sunshine
- dry weather
- rainstorms
- windblown dust

How would a **drought** affect you if your family was planning a camping or fishing trip at a lake?

A Word a Day, Primary • EMC 2717 • ©2002 by Evan-Moor Corp.

fragile

adjective

Something **fragile** is delicate and easily broken.

The **fragile** vase broke when it fell on the tile floor.

Which words mean about the same thing as **fragile**?

- weak
- tough
- strong
- breakable
- indestructible

How do you feel when you are around lots of **fragile** objects? How do you act?

spectacular

adjective

Something that is unusually amazing is **spectacular**.

The glowing orange sunset was the most **spectacular** I'd ever seen.

Which of these is probably **spectacular**?

- a paper clip
- a mud puddle
- a fireworks show
- a double rainbow
- a New Year's Day parade

Tell about the most **spectacular** thing you've ever seen or would like to see.

A Word a Day

scold

verb

When you **scold** someone, you speak sharply about something.

The teacher had to **scold** the class for their rude behavior during the assembly.

Which statements might parents make when they **scold** their child?

- "Your room looks terrific!"
- "You know better than that!"
- "Please don't ever do that again!"
- "You did a great job on that report!"
- "How many times have I asked you not to do that?"

Tell about a time when you or someone you know got **scolded** for something. What happened?

considerate

adjective

A **considerate** person is thoughtful and kind to others.

The **considerate** boy brought his mother tea when she was sick in bed.

Which of these show **considerate** behavior?

- pushing in line
- sending a get-well card
- yelling at someone who bothers you
- helping to clear the dishes after dinner
- offering to show a new student around the school

Tell about a time when someone was **considerate** to you. How did that make you feel?

A Word a Day, Primary • EMC 2717 • ©2002 by Evan-Moor Corp.

blizzard

noun

A **blizzard** is a very heavy snowstorm.

After the **blizzard**, we had to dig our car out from under a pile of snow.

Which of these would you expect during a **blizzard**?

- ice on the windows
- freezing cold air
- bright sunshine
- a warm breeze
- a strong wind

What would you need to be prepared in case you were caught in a **blizzard**?

instruct

verb

When you **instruct**, you teach something to someone.

My uncle is a lifeguard, so he can **instruct** me on pool safety.

Which of the following mean about the same thing as **instruct**?

- train
- tutor
- learn
- coach
- study

Think about a special skill or talent you have. How would you **instruct** others so they could also learn this skill?

A Word a Day

canine

noun

An animal that belongs to the dog family is a **canine**.

It's not hard to see that dogs and wolves are both **canines**.

Which of the following belong to a **canine**?

- fur
- claws
- scales
- fangs
- feathers

If you owned a **canine**, would you prefer a dog or a tame wolf?

increase

verb

You **increase** something when you make or get more of it.

My dad said he'd **increase** my allowance if I started doing more chores.

In which of these situations is something being **increased**?

- The principal makes recess ten minutes longer.
- Mom gives me two cookies instead of three.
- I use a pump to add more air to my bike tires.
- We get 100 new books for the school library.
- Dad slows the car down for a stoplight.

What would you like to **increase** at school so that you'd have more of it?

A Word a Day, Primary • EMC 2717 • ©2002 by Evan-Moor Corp.

annual

adjective

An **annual** event happens one time a year.

Our family gathers every June for the **annual** Chávez family reunion.

Which of the following are **annual** events?

- Saturday
- a rainy day
- your birthday
- New Year's Day
- the Fourth of July

What's your favorite **annual** event? What do you like about it?

orbit

noun

The path that the Earth or a planet travels in around the Sun is its **orbit**.

Scientists can observe the **orbit** of distant planets.

Which of these has an **orbit**?

- a planet
- the Sun
- Mercury
- a balloon
- the ocean

What tools might scientists use to follow a planet's **orbit**?

A Word a Day

eager

adjective

If you're excited and can't wait to do something, you're **eager**.

The **eager** children couldn't wait to get on the bus and go to the zoo.

Would you be **eager** if

- you were going to the toy store?
- it was your day to do all the chores?
- it was time to open your birthday gifts?
- it was the first day of summer vacation?
- you had to go to bed an hour earlier than usual?

Tell about a time when you were very **eager** to do something. How did you pass the time until it was time to do that activity?

commence

verb

When you **commence**, you begin something.

When the players are done warming up, the ball game will **commence**.

Which of these mean about the same thing as **commence**?

- stop
- start
- halt
- get going
- finish

When do you **commence** to get ready for bed on school nights?

A Word a Day, Primary • EMC 2717 • ©2002 by Evan-Moor Corp.

locate

verb

You **locate** something when you find it.

I couldn't **locate** my favorite shirt, but then I found it in a basket of clean laundry.

Where would you **locate**

- your bike?
- your shoes?
- your backpack?
- your favorite toy?
- your homework?

What do you do when you can't **locate** something that you need?

possession

noun

Something that belongs to you is your **possession**.

I keep my **possessions** on my side of the room, and my sister keeps hers on her side.

To whom do each of these **possessions** belong?

- the car
- your house
- your backpack
- your brush and comb
- your best friend's bike

Tell about one of your favorite **possessions**. Where did you get it and how do you care for it?

A Word a Day

significant

adjective

If something is **significant**, it has importance.

My mom writes about all the **significant** events in my life in my baby book: my first steps, my first loose tooth, my first day at school, and others.

Which of these is **significant**?

- turning 90 years old
- changing a light bulb
- graduating from high school
- riding a bike alone for the first time
- eating a peanut butter and jelly sandwich

Tell about a **significant** event in your life and how it changed you or those around you.

ascend

verb

When you **ascend**, you go up.

The airplane took off and **ascended** through the clouds.

Which of these could you **ascend**?

- a rug
- a ladder
- the stairs
- a mountain
- a birthday cake

Imagine you have just **ascended** in a hot-air balloon or hang glider. Describe what you think the view is from up in the sky.

A Word a Day, Primary • EMC 2717 • ©2002 by Evan-Moor Corp.

browse

verb

You **browse** when you look at something in a quick, casual way.

My mom didn't want to buy any books at the bookstore; she just wanted to **browse**.

Which of these mean about the same thing as **browse**?

- scan
- skim
- study
- glance
- examine

Tell about something you like to **browse** through.

cautious

adjective

When you're very careful and don't take any chances, you're being **cautious**.

We had to be **cautious** on the way to school because of all the road work.

In which of these situations should you be **cautious**?

- when you eat a cookie
- when you pour hot liquid
- when you use a sharp knife
- when you quietly read a book
- when you cross a busy street

Tell about a time when you had to be **cautious** about something. What did you do and how did it turn out?

A Word a Day

elderly

adjective

A senior citizen or older person is **elderly**.

The **elderly** woman was 85 when she took her first airplane trip!

Which of these could describe an **elderly** person?

- wise
- cruel
- athletic
- experienced
- white-haired

Tell about something you've learned from an **elderly** person.

eliminate

verb

If you get rid of something, you **eliminate** it.

After we rake the leaves, we can **eliminate** that chore from our list.

Which of these would you like to **eliminate**?

- recess
- homework
- washing dishes
- after-school snacks
- making your bed every day

If you could **eliminate** one thing from your day, what would it be and why?

A Word a Day, Primary • EMC 2717 • ©2002 by Evan-Moor Corp.

avoid

verb

You **avoid** something if you try to stay away from it or keep it from happening.

Jenny **avoided** me at school because she'd borrowed my book and forgot to return it.

Which of these would you probably **avoid**?

- getting a birthday present
- a baseball hit in your direction
- showing your parents an excellent report card
- stepping in a mud puddle if you're wearing sandals
- riding your bike on the sidewalk where a child is playing

If you could **avoid** doing one thing, what would it be and why?

stoop

verb

You **stoop** when you squat down.

Natalie had to **stoop** to pick up the pencil that she dropped on the floor.

Would you have to **stoop** to

- reach the highest book on the shelf?
- pick up the cat dish to fill it with water?
- pick up the newspaper in the driveway?
- pick up a baby bird that fell from its nest?
- catch a balloon that floated up and away?

What is something in your classroom that you have to **stoop** to reach?

A Word a Day

transparent

adjective

Something is **transparent** if light goes through it and you can see through it.

We watched the fish at the aquarium through a large **transparent** window.

Which of the following are **transparent**?

- a brick
- a book
- a fishbowl
- a window
- a pair of glasses

What do you have that's **transparent**? What is it made of?

accurate

adjective

Something is **accurate** if it has no mistakes.

John was **accurate** in his spelling of all the words and got an A on his test.

In which of these situations is it important to be **accurate**?

- giving change to a customer
- putting a jigsaw puzzle together
- taking pills that the doctor prescribed
- throwing clothing in the laundry basket
- giving your address to the 911 operator during a home emergency

What is something that you must be absolutely **accurate** about? What would happen if you weren't?

A Word a Day, Primary • EMC 2717 • ©2002 by Evan-Moor Corp.

fiction

noun

Fiction is writing that tells about characters and places that are make-believe.

I wrote a story about a princess and a magic chicken for the **fiction** contest.

Which of the following are examples of **fiction**?

- the story of "The Three Little Pigs"
- a book about a talking duck
- the life story of Abraham Lincoln
- a book of facts about snakes and lizards
- the story of how electricity was discovered

What's your favorite **fiction** story? Why do you like it? Do you prefer **fiction** or nonfiction when you choose something to read? Why?

irritable

adjective

An **irritable** person is grumpy and gets mad easily.

I get **irritable** when I'm tired and hungry; it's best to leave me alone when I'm like that!

Would you be **irritable** if

- mosquitoes were stinging you?
- your favorite movie was on TV?
- you were going out for ice cream?
- your baby sister spilled milk all over you?
- you were trying to read and someone kept interrupting you?

What makes you get **irritable**? What do you do when you start feeling that way? What makes you feel better?

A Word a Day

mob

noun

A **mob** is a large, disorderly crowd.

Police officers tried to control the **mob** that was waiting for the rock star to arrive.

Which of these is a **mob**?

- your family at the dinner table
- a child feeding a duck at the park
- a crowd of shoppers waiting for the doors to open at the mall
- two children sharing a sandwich on the bench at school recess
- a large group of people waiting to buy tickets at the opening of baseball season

Tell about a time when you've seen a **mob**. What were they doing? How might it be dangerous to be in or near a **mob**?

launch

verb

When you set a vehicle in motion into the water or air, you **launch** it.

The **launch** of the space shuttle is planned for a clear day.

Which of these could you **launch**?

- a cup
- a car
- a ship
- a rocket
- a telephone

Have you ever built something and **launched** it? If so, tell about it. If not, what would you like to make and **launch**?

A Word a Day, Primary • EMC 2717 • ©2002 by Evan-Moor Corp.

frequent

adjective

If something happens often, it's **frequent**.

We couldn't hear what our teacher was saying because of the **frequent** interruptions.

Which of these is **frequent**?

- a lot
- once a year
- every ten years
- once every minute
- every five minutes

Tell about a time when you were trying to do something and had **frequent** interruptions. What happened? How did you feel?

fidgety

adjective

Someone who is **fidgety** has trouble staying still.

The toddlers could only sit still for ten minutes before they got **fidgety**.

Which of these mean about the same thing as **fidgety**?

- restless
- squirmy
- nervous
- calm
- still

When have you felt yourself getting **fidgety**? What can you do when you get **fidgety**?

A Word a Day

independent

adjective

When you think and act for yourself, you're being **independent**.

Even though my grandma is over 90 years old, she is still totally **independent**.

Would you be **independent** if you

- had your best friend choose the color of your new bike?
- finished your homework by yourself?
- needed help to make your bed?
- make your own breakfast?
- choose your own clothes?

In what ways are you **independent**? In what ways can't you be **independent** yet?

refuse

verb

If you say no to something, you **refuse** it.

When he was asked to baby-sit, Martin **refused** because he was too exhausted.

Which statements could be used to **refuse** something?

- "No, I won't."
- "Sure, I'd love to go."
- "I'd never try to do that by myself."
- "I'll go to the party with you."
- "Sorry, but I don't eat meat."

Tell about a time when you **refused** to do something. What happened? When is it a good idea to **refuse** to do something? When isn't it such a good idea?

A Word a Day, Primary • EMC 2717 • ©2002 by Evan-Moor Corp.

inflate

verb

If you fill something with air or gas, you **inflate** it.

The coach forgot to **inflate** the ball, so it was too flat to bounce.

Which of these could you **inflate**?

- a table
- a football
- a baseball
- a telephone
- a hot-air balloon

Have you ever **inflated** a ball, balloon, or bike tire? Did you use a pump or your lungs? Tell about how the thing you were **inflating** changed.

adjustable

adjective

Something is **adjustable** if it can be changed to make it fit or work better.

The **adjustable** chair could go up for taller people and down for shorter people.

Which of these is **adjustable**?

- a belt
- a sock
- a radio
- an earring
- an antenna

What article of clothing do you have that's **adjustable**? What furniture or appliances do you have that are **adjustable**? In what ways are they **adjustable**?

A Word a Day

astonish

verb

If you greatly surprise someone, you **astonish** them.

We were **astonished** when the magician pulled ten rabbits out of his hat.

Would it **astonish** you to see someone

- yawn?
- shot out of a cannon?
- brush their teeth?
- walk on their hands?
- twist their body into a pretzel shape?

Tell about a time when something **astonished** you. What was it and how did you feel?

statement

noun

You make a **statement** when you say something.

Everyone waited for the president to make a **statement** about the peace agreement.

Which of the following are **statements**?

- "Can we go?"
- "I don't like spinach."
- "My favorite color is red."
- "I have a new baby sister."
- "Would you like some ice cream?"

Make a **statement** about what you like best in school. Now ask someone else to make a **statement**.

A Word a Day, Primary • EMC 2717 • ©2002 by Evan-Moor Corp.

charity

noun

A **charity** is a group that collects money or things to help needy people.

The children gave their toys to a **charity** that sends them to sick children.

Which of the following could you give to a **charity** to help others?

- clothes
- one old sock
- used furniture
- games and toys
- a piece of bubble gum

If you could organize a drive to give things to a **charity**, what would you want to collect and what **charity** would you give them to?

disposable

adjective

Something is **disposable** if you can throw it away after using it.

It's better for the environment to use cloth towels instead of **disposable** paper towels to clean up spills.

Which of the following are **disposable**?

- bed sheets
- computers
- paper napkins
- paper diapers
- paper drinking cups

What do you have in your lunch that's **disposable**? What do you have that can be recycled? Do you think it's better for our planet to use **disposable** or recyclable things?

A Word a Day

ancient

adjective

If something is **ancient**, it is extremely old.

The king wore an **ancient** crown that had been handed down in his family for generations.

Which of these might be displayed at a museum of **ancient** history?

- a fossil
- a computer game
- a solar-powered car
- a statue of a Roman emperor
- stones from a temple built 6,000 years ago

What is something **ancient** that you have seen? Where did you see it?

fragrance

noun

A **fragrance** is a sweet, pleasant smell.

The warm sunshine released a lovely **fragrance** from the blooming jasmine.

Which of these has a **fragrance**?

- water
- a rose
- a skunk
- perfume
- freshly baked cookies

What **fragrance** do you enjoy? Do you prefer the **fragrance** of perfume or the natural **fragrance** of flowers?

A Word a Day, Primary • EMC 2717 • ©2002 by Evan-Moor Corp.

vanish

verb

If you disappear suddenly, you **vanish**.

The moon **vanished** behind the clouds.

Which of these mean about the same thing as **vanish**?

- go
- leave
- appear
- show up
- fade away

If you had the power to make one thing **vanish** so the world would become a better place, what would you choose?

reasonable

adjective

Something **reasonable** is fair and makes sense.

I think eight dollars is a **reasonable** price for a haircut.

Would it be **reasonable** to

- only eat dessert?
- keep an elephant as a pet?
- sleep only two hours each night?
- wear a warm jacket in the winter?
- eat a good breakfast before school?

Tell about a time when someone asked you to do something that was **reasonable**. Now think of a time when someone expected something that was not **reasonable**. What did you do?

A Word a Day

anticipate

verb

If you **anticipate** something, you expect it to happen and are prepared for it.

The weather forecast said to **anticipate** a storm, so we got our rain gear ready.

Which events might you want to **anticipate** and be prepared for?

- a power outage
- the daily mail delivery
- a difficult spelling test
- your cousins' annual visit
- a flood of the nearby river

What is something you **anticipate** each year, and how do you get ready for it?

withdraw

verb

When you **withdraw** something, you take it away or remove it.

I'm not allowed to **withdraw** money from my savings account in the bank; I can only add money to it.

Which words mean about the same thing as **withdraw**?

- draw
- enter
- pull out
- take out
- take over

Have you ever joined a class or another activity, but then had to **withdraw**? If not, how do you think it would feel to be in that situation?

A Word a Day, Primary • EMC 2717 • ©2002 by Evan-Moor Corp.

unfortunate

adjective

Something that is **unfortunate** is unlucky.

It was **unfortunate** that Abby forgot to bring her swimsuit to the pool.

Which of the following situations are **unfortunate**?

- getting a new puppy
- winning the schoolwide spelling bee
- your house catching on fire and burning up
- getting home too late to stay up and finish your book
- forgetting to turn in the homework that you worked so hard to complete

Tell about a time when something **unfortunate** happened to you or someone you know. How did you feel?

banquet

noun

A **banquet** is a big formal meal for a large group of people on a special occasion.

The chef prepared lots of food and a beautiful cake for the wedding **banquet**.

Which of the following might you see at a **banquet**?

- beautiful china dishes
- fine silverware
- crystal goblets
- take-out food
- paper cups

Have you ever been to a **banquet**? How is a **banquet** different from dinner at your house?

A Word a Day

babble

verb

When you **babble**, you make sounds that don't have any meaning.

When the baby started to **babble**, we knew it wouldn't be long before she'd say her first real words.

Which ones might **babble**?

- a television newscaster
- a teacher giving a spelling test
- a chimp that is mimicking a person
- a person pretending to speak another language
- someone who is so scared that he can barely speak

Tell about a time when you were so scared, nervous, or excited that you started to **babble**. Why is it hard to understand someone who **babbles**?

hubbub

noun

A **hubbub** is a loud, confused situation.

The blue jays made such a **hubbub** outside my window that they woke me up.

Which of these would make a **hubbub**?

- a purring cat
- a pack of barking dogs
- workers drilling in the street
- a snake gliding through tall grass
- three-year-olds at a birthday party

Tell about a time when you made a **hubbub**. What was going on? What did you do?

A Word a Day, Primary • EMC 2717 • ©2002 by Evan-Moor Corp.

ancestor

noun

An **ancestor** is a family member who lived long ago, even before your grandparents.

My mother's **ancestors** came from Spain and my father's were from Russia.

Which of the following could be an **ancestor**?

- your sister
- your cousin
- your best friend
- your great-grandfather
- your great-great-great aunt

Tell something you know about your **ancestors**, or share something you'd like to learn about them.

quarrel

verb

If you **quarrel** with someone, you argue or fight.

My brother and I usually get along, but sometimes we **quarrel** over our chores.

Which of these mean about the same thing as **quarrel**?

- fight
- share
- agree
- argue
- disagree

Tell about a time when you **quarreled** with someone. How did it end? How did you work it out?

A Word a Day

prompt

adjective

Someone who is **prompt** is always on time.

A **prompt** student is always in class when the bell rings.

Would it be important to be **prompt** if you

- have a doctor's appointment?
- have to catch a plane for a trip?
- want to see the beginning of a movie?
- can water the plants anytime during the day?
- are going to a school carnival that is going on all day long?

Are you **prompt** in getting to school every day? Why is this important? What happens if you aren't **prompt** in getting to school?

motion

noun

Motion is any kind of movement.

The rocking **motion** of the ship made it hard to walk without falling.

Which of these is in **motion**?

- your desk
- a parked car
- a rocking chair
- a dog chasing a ball
- a kite blowing in the wind

Has a **motion** ever made you feel dizzy or sick? If so, what sort of **motion** was it?

A Word a Day, Primary • EMC 2717 • ©2002 by Evan-Moor Corp.

encourage

verb

If you give someone courage or hope, you **encourage** them.

Jill didn't think she could finish the race, but her coach **encouraged** her and she made it!

Which statements would someone make to **encourage** you?

- "You might as well just give up."
- "That's the way to go!"
- "Hang in there!"
- "You can do it."
- "Forget it."

Tell about a time that you weren't sure you could do something and someone **encouraged** you to try. Who **encouraged** you and what happened?

halt

verb

When you **halt**, you come to a stop.

The police officer had the cars **halt** so that the man in the wheelchair could cross the street safely.

In which of these situations would you **halt**?

- at the park
- at a red light
- at a stop sign
- at a yellow light
- when you hear the siren of an emergency vehicle

Why is it important to **halt** when you come to a stop sign, red light, or hear an emergency siren? What would happen if you didn't **halt**?

A Word a Day

demand

verb

You **demand** something when you ask for it firmly or order it to be done.

The teacher **demanded** to know who threw the paper airplane.

Which of these statements is a **demand**?

- "Mind me this instant!"
- "Stop that immediately."
- "Am I invited to the party, too?"
- "You must tell me right now."
- "Yes, you may have more ice cream."

How is a **demand** different than asking someone a question nicely? Which do you prefer and why? How do you feel when someone makes a **demand** of you?

pollution

noun

Pollution dirties the pure air, water, and land of our planet.

Electric and solar-powered cars are good for our planet because they don't create air **pollution**.

Which of the following might cause **pollution**?

- rain
- a rainbow
- exhaust from cars
- oil spilled from a tanker in the ocean
- chemicals from a factory that leak into the ground

What can people do to help stop **pollution**? What are some things that you do?

A Word a Day, Primary • EMC 2717 • ©2002 by Evan-Moor Corp.

applaud

verb

You **applaud** by clapping your hands to show that you liked something.

The crowd **applauded** when the firefighter brought the child out of the building.

Would you **applaud** for

- the winner of the school spelling bee?
- your dinner?
- a singer at the end of a song?
- the actors at the end of a play?
- the mail carrier?

Tell about a time when you **applauded** for something. Has anyone ever **applauded** for you? If so, how did you feel?

tattered

adjective

Something is **tattered** if it's old and torn.

Among the things in Great-grandma's trunk in the attic were some **tattered** clothes and antique jewelry.

Which words mean about the same thing as **tattered**?

- new
- torn
- whole
- ripped
- shredded

Tell about something you or your family have that is **tattered**, but is still precious to you. Why is it special?

A Word a Day

exhausted

adjective

When you are extremely tired, you're **exhausted**.

We were **exhausted** after hiking uphill all day long.

Would you be **exhausted** if you

- ran a long race?
- went to bed early and slept late?
- worked at a school car wash all day?
- stayed up all night with a bad cough?
- sat on the porch reading and sipping lemonade?

Tell about a time when you felt **exhausted** and couldn't stay awake. What can you do to be sure you don't feel **exhausted** while you're in school?

observe

verb

You **observe** something when you watch or study it carefully.

An astronomer **observes** the stars to learn and teach others about them.

Which of these mean about the same thing as **observe**?

- examine
- look at
- notice
- plan
- see

What can you **observe** from where you sit in the classroom? What can you **observe** from a window in your house?

A Word a Day, Primary • EMC 2717 • ©2002 by Evan-Moor Corp.

function

noun

The purpose or job of someone or something is its **function**.

The **function** of the microwave oven is to cook or heat food.

What is the **function** of

- a book?
- a bicycle?
- a teacher?
- a newspaper?
- a refrigerator?

Do students in your class have any special **functions**? What are they? What about the adults who work at your school? What **functions** do they perform?

convenient

adjective

Something is **convenient** if it's useful, easy, and no trouble.

It's very **convenient** to heat food in a microwave oven because it's so fast.

Would it be **convenient** if

- a book you needed was too high to reach?
- someone interrupted you while you were studying?
- the bus you rode stopped right in front of your house?
- the supermarket stayed open twenty-four hours a day?
- your baseball game was at the same time as your brother's?

Tell about something you use at home that's **convenient** for you to reach. Is there something that isn't **convenient** that you need help to get?

A Word a Day

postpone

verb

When you **postpone** something, you put it off until later.

We had to **postpone** the picnic until the weekend because of the rain.

Which of the following mean about the same thing as **postpone**?

- delay
- do now
- reschedule
- begin immediately
- change to another day

Tell about a time when you had to **postpone** something you were planning to do. Why did you have to **postpone** it? Were you able to reschedule it?

discourage

verb

You **discourage** someone if you try to convince him or her not to do something.

My dad **discouraged** us from climbing the tree because it was too high.

Which statements could you make to **discourage** someone?

- "I don't think that makes much sense."
- "I don't think you should try that."
- "Keep up the good work!"
- "That's not a good idea."
- "Go for it!"

When has someone **discouraged** you from doing something? What was his or her reason? How did you feel?

A Word a Day, Primary • EMC 2717 • ©2002 by Evan-Moor Corp.

unusual

adjective

If something is different or strange, it's **unusual**.

It was **unusual** for my dad to be home at 3 o'clock in the afternoon instead of around dinnertime.

Would it be **unusual**

- to learn to ride a bike?
- to see a two-headed dog?
- to read a book backwards?
- to see a clown at the circus?
- for tennis balls to fall from the sky?

Tell about something **unusual** that happened to you or someone you know.

audience

noun

A group of people who watch a show or performance is an **audience**.

The **audience** clapped to let the actors know they enjoyed the play.

At which of these would you find an **audience**?

- at a musical program
- listening to a speech
- at the grocery store
- in your kitchen
- at the movies

Tell about a time you were a member of an **audience**. What are some polite rules of behavior when you're in an **audience**?

A Word a Day

anxious

adjective

If you are **anxious** to do something, you are waiting eagerly for it to happen.

Kim was **anxious** for the circus to come to town because she loved to watch the trapeze artists.

Would you be **anxious**

- to catch a bad cold?
- to have your bike stolen?
- for your birthday to come?
- to go to an amusement park?
- for your best friend to spend the night?

Tell about a time when you were **anxious** for something to happen. What were you waiting for? How did you get through the days of waiting?

cooperate

verb

When people work together toward a common goal, they **cooperate**.

If we all **cooperate**, we can clean up the class very quickly.

Which words might be spoken by someone who knows how to **cooperate**?

- "I'll help you with that."
- "Let's do this together."
- "I really don't need you."
- "Please leave me alone."
- "There's room for everyone to help."

What kinds of things do people in your family do to **cooperate** at home? How does this help everyone to get along?

A Word a Day, Primary • EMC 2717 • ©2002 by Evan-Moor Corp.

solution

noun

A **solution** is the answer or explanation for a problem or question.

The detective found the **solution** to the mystery by studying the clues.

Which of these has a **solution**?

- a riddle
- a puzzle
- your name
- a mystery story
- a phone number

Think of a time you had a problem. How did you find the **solution**? Have you ever helped someone find the **solution** to his or her problem? How did it make you feel?

knowledge

noun

Knowledge is what you know and what you learn.

My science teacher loves sharing her **knowledge** of nature with us.

What special **knowledge** would you need in order to do the job done by each of these workers?

- ball player
- gardener
- teacher
- doctor
- artist

How does the **knowledge** that you get in school help? How do you think it might help you in the future?

A Word a Day

rapid

adjective

Something that's very fast is **rapid**.

My heartbeat became very **rapid** after I ran a mile.

Which words mean about the same thing as **rapid**?

- slow
- swift
- quick
- speedy
- crawling

Is your breathing **rapid** or slow right now? When does it become **rapid**? How does that feel?

nonsense

noun

Nonsense is something silly that has little or no meaning.

It's **nonsense** to think you can fly if you jump up high enough.

Which sentences are **nonsense**?

- Yesterday I invited an elephant home for lunch.
- The moon is made of green cheese.
- It's important to eat a good breakfast.
- I can hold my breath for three days.
- A baby cat is called a kitten.

What's something that you've heard that you knew was absolute **nonsense**? Do you ever enjoy **nonsense**? Why?

A Word a Day, Primary • EMC 2717 • ©2002 by Evan-Moor Corp.

passenger

noun

A **passenger** rides in a vehicle driven or piloted by another person.

The **passengers** had to wait for the pilot to park the plane to unbuckle their seat belts.

Which of these should a **passenger** do?

- tickle the driver
- wear a seat belt
- help watch for street signs
- throw things out the window
- let the driver concentrate on driving

What are some games you can play when you're a **passenger** in a car to make the time go by quickly?

struggle

verb

When you work hard at something that is difficult, you **struggle**.

I had to **struggle** to learn my spelling words, but now I never misspell them.

Which of these might you do if you **struggle** with something?

- give up
- try harder
- do it over again
- get help from someone
- get it perfect the first time

What do you **struggle** to do well? What's easy for you to do well?

A Word a Day

stubborn

adjective

If you are **stubborn**, you like to do things your way and not give up on your ideas.

The **stubborn** child refused to let go of the ball in the toy store.

Which of the following might a **stubborn** person say?

- "I will not go to bed."
- "That's fine; we can try it your way."
- "I don't want vanilla; I only want chocolate."
- "I don't care what you say; it wasn't my fault."
- "You're right; I guess I can change my plans."

Do you know anybody who is **stubborn**? What do you do to get along with that person? Are you ever **stubborn**? About what? Is it ever a good idea to be **stubborn**?

conduct

noun

Your **conduct** is the way you act or behave.

The children's **conduct** at the assembly was so good that they got extra recess time.

In which of these places should your **conduct** be calm and quiet?

- in class
- at the park
- in a meeting
- at the library
- at a birthday party

Tell about a time when you got a compliment from a parent, friend, or teacher because of your good **conduct**. What happens if your class's **conduct** is not appropriate?

characteristic

noun

A **characteristic** is a quality or feature that someone or something has.

A long neck is one of the giraffe's most noticeable **characteristics**.

Name a noticeable **characteristic** for each of the following:

- an elephant
- a banana
- a turtle
- snow
- you

What **characteristics** do you have that are similar to those of someone else in your family? What **characteristics** do you have that are different?

cherish

verb

When you **cherish** someone or something, you treasure it in a special way.

My mother **cherishes** the tea set her mother gave her when she was a little girl.

Which of the following might someone **cherish**?

- old photos of Grandpa as a baby
- Mom's wedding gown
- a sour pickle
- an award
- dust

Tell about something you **cherish**, how you got it, and why it's so special to you.

A Word a Day

expand

verb

When you **expand** something, you make it bigger.

You could see the flat tire **expand** as air was pumped in.

Which of these could you **expand**?

- a brick
- a circle
- a balloon
- a page in a book
- a collection of toy cars

Are you wearing anything that can **expand**? Check around your waist, cuffs, or neck.

edible

adjective

Something that can be eaten is **edible**.

Rhubarb stalks are **edible**, but their leaves can be poisonous.

Which of the following are **edible**?

- mud
- snails
- chicken
- crayons
- strawberries

Can you always tell if plants growing in the wild are **edible**? Do you think it's a good idea to try things to find out?

A Word a Day, Primary • EMC 2717 • ©2002 by Evan-Moor Corp.

ingredients

noun

Ingredients are what you combine to make something else.

Rick put all the **ingredients** for the cookies into the bowl while I stirred them.

Which of the following would be an **ingredient** for cake?

- flour
- eggs
- sugar
- ground beef
- tomato sauce

What are the **ingredients** for your favorite sandwich? Why does a recipe list **ingredients**?

destination

noun

The place that someone or something is going is the **destination**.

This year the **destination** for our family vacation is Hawai`i.

Which of the following would probably be a great vacation **destination**?

- a sunny beach
- a lakeside cabin
- near an active volcano
- near an amusement park
- on the shores of a polluted river

What is the farthest **destination** you have visited? Did you travel there by train, ship, plane, or car?

A Word a Day

landscape

noun

A **landscape** is a painting of natural outdoor scenery.

The museum had a special exhibit of **landscape** paintings this spring.

Which of the following might you see in a **landscape**?

- trees
- highrises
- the ocean
- a freeway
- mountains

Why do you think artists paint **landscapes**? Why do you think people enjoy looking at **landscapes**?

youth

noun

You are a **youth** after childhood and before adulthood.

My grandpa delivered newspapers on his bicycle when he was a **youth**.

Which of these is a **youth**?

- your great-aunt
- your grandmother
- your teenage cousin
- your 16-year-old brother
- your 14-year-old baby-sitter

Tell about something your mom or dad did when they were **youths**. How were things different for them than for **youths** today?

A Word a Day, Primary • EMC 2717 • ©2002 by Evan-Moor Corp.

verdict

noun

A **verdict** is a decision made by a jury.

The twelve members of the jury discussed the case for hours before reaching a guilty **verdict**.

Which words mean about the same thing as **verdict**?

- ruling
- finding
- judgment
- argument
- disappointment

Do you think that someday you would like to be part of a jury and help reach a **verdict** in a case?

theme

noun

A **theme** is the topic or subject of something.

Ana's party had a rainforest **theme**, so all the party favors were rainforest animal toys.

Which of the following could have a **theme**?

- a party
- a book
- a couch
- a movie
- a hairbrush

What was the **theme** of the last book you read? What **theme** do you find most interesting?

A Word a Day

strive

verb

When you **strive**, you make your best effort to do something.

I **strive** to walk a little farther every day on my morning walk.

Which words would a coach say if he wanted his players to **strive** to play their best game?

- "Give up when it gets hard."

- "Do your best."

- "Try hard."

- "Run away."

- "Make every effort."

What do you **strive** to do well at home? How about in school? What do you **strive** to do in a sport or hobby?

similar

adjective

Two things are **similar** if they are very much alike.

My brother and I like **similar** sports, but the books we like are totally different.

Which pairs of words name things that are **similar**?

- a basketball and a soccer ball

- a shoe and a slipper

- a radio and a bed

- a piano and a lamp

- a pond and a lagoon

Tell about how you are **similar** to your mom or dad, to a brother or sister, or to your best friend.

A Word a Day, Primary • EMC 2717 • ©2002 by Evan-Moor Corp.

thorough

adjective

When something is **thorough**, it is done carefully and completely from start to finish.

Grace did such a **thorough** job cleaning that there wasn't a speck of dust left.

Which of these describe people doing a **thorough** job?

- Anthony stopped doing chores to play ball.
- Ben studied for two hours without a break.
- Without the directions, the boys couldn't complete the model.
- Laurel soon gave up on learning her new piano piece.
- Mom and Josh washed, dried, and put away all the dishes.

Tell about a time when you did a **thorough** job. What were the steps you followed, from start to finish? How did you feel afterward? Was there ever a time when you didn't do a **thorough** job? What happened?

appetite

noun

Your **appetite** is your hunger for food.

I'm not allowed to have snacks after four o'clock so I won't spoil my **appetite** for dinner.

Which of the following appeal to your **appetite**?

- rich, dark chocolate cake
- hot buttered popcorn
- strong, black coffee
- tart, crunchy apples
- spicy chili

What kind of food do you have a big **appetite** for? How do you feel when you can't satisfy your **appetite**?

A Word a Day

content

adjective

When you are **content**, you are happy and satisfied.

The kitten was so **content** as she drank her milk that she began purring.

Which words mean about the same thing as **content**?

- glad
- upset
- pleased
- dissatisfied
- displeased

What makes you **content**? Do you usually feel **content** or not?

parched

adjective

You are **parched** if you are extremely hot and dry and need water.

We ran out of water and were totally **parched** by the time we crossed the desert.

Which of these mean about the same thing as **parched**?

- moist
- damp
- dried out
- withered
- dehydrated

Tell about a time when you were **parched**. What did you do? What happens to plants when they're **parched**?

A Word a Day, Primary • EMC 2717 • ©2002 by Evan-Moor Corp.

qualify

verb

You **qualify** for something if you meet all the necessary requirements.

Our team had to win three games in order to **qualify** to go on to the finals.

Which activities would you need to **qualify** for?

- making your bed
- teaching in an elementary school
- joining the young people's orchestra
- competing as a gymnast in the Olympics
- representing your school at a statewide spelling bee

Imagine you are offering to walk your neighbor's dog. What would you say to convince him or her that you **qualify** to do this job?

quench

verb

When you **quench** your thirst, you drink something refreshing.

On a hot summer's day, there's nothing like ice-cold lemonade to **quench** my thirst.

In which of these situations might you need to **quench** your thirst?

- while you're sleeping
- after eating salty chips
- after running a long race
- when working out in the garden
- sitting on the beach under a hot sun

What is your favorite thing to drink when you need to **quench** your thirst?

A Word a Day

opponent

noun

An **opponent** is someone who is trying to beat you in a contest or an election.

Sue's **opponent** in the tennis match scored the last point and won the trophy.

Which of the following could be an **opponent**?

- the person you're trying to beat at checkers
- the person you're working with on a class project
- the person running against you for class president
- the person who is teaching you how to play the piano
- the person who's trying to kick the ball into the goal that you're defending

Why is it important to show your **opponent** that you are a good sport?

opportunity

noun

An **opportunity** is a chance for something.

My dad has the **opportunity** to get a great new job, so we might have to move.

Which of the following offer you an **opportunity**?

- drinking a glass of water
- being asked to join the Scouts
- getting an invitation to a birthday party
- putting your dirty clothes in the laundry basket
- receiving an offer to try out for the gymnastics team

What special **opportunity** has been made available to you? Did you take advantage of that **opportunity**? What happened?

A Word a Day, Primary • EMC 2717 • ©2002 by Evan-Moor Corp.

advise

verb

When you **advise** someone, you give suggestions that will help him or her make a decision.

Jamie **advised** me to buy the red shirt because it went better with my jacket.

What would you **advise** a friend who

- lost a dollar on the playground?
- accidentally broke their mom's vase?
- wanted to play ball with you but had chores to do?
- wanted to buy a new toy but didn't have enough money?
- was afraid to tell the teacher about losing a book?

Tell about a time when you **advised** someone about something, or a time when someone **advised** you. How did it turn out?

positive

adjective

You're **positive** about something when you are absolutely certain of it.

I'm **positive** I left my coat on the playground because I took it off to swing on the bars.

Which statements show that the speaker is **positive** about something?

- "I'm not sure."
- "I know that for a fact."
- "I have no doubt about it."
- "I really haven't made up my mind yet."
- "I give you my word that you can count on me."

What is something that you are absolutely **positive** about? How do you know for sure?

A Word a Day

peer

noun

A person who is in your age group is a **peer**.

Mario worked with a group of his **peers** to clean up the school garden.

Which ones could be your **peer**?

- your dentist
- your best friend
- the school secretary
- the child sitting next to you in class
- another player on your baseball team

Tell about a time when you and a **peer** did a fun activity together, helped each other, or worked on a project. Why is it fun to work with a **peer**?

satisfactory

adjective

Something that is good enough is **satisfactory**.

Her first book report was **satisfactory**, but the next one she wrote was outstanding.

Which of the following mean about the same thing as **satisfactory**?

- okay
- passing
- acceptable
- outstanding
- unacceptable

Tell about a time when you did something that was **satisfactory**, but the next time you improved and did an outstanding job.

A Word a Day, Primary • EMC 2717 • ©2002 by Evan-Moor Corp.

respond

verb

When you answer or reply, you **respond**.

The invitation said to **respond** by calling if you planned to attend the party.

How would you **respond** if

- your mother asks if you want more dessert?
- your best friend wants you to come over and play?
- your brother asks if he can borrow your favorite toy?
- someone calls to talk to your dad, but he's at work?
- your teacher asks for a volunteer to take a note to the office?

Have you ever had to **respond** to an invitation? Did you **respond** by phone, in writing, or in person? What is a polite way to **respond** if you cannot accept the invitation?

request

verb

When you ask for something politely, you **request** it.

Margo called the radio to **request** that they play her favorite song, and they did!

How would you **request** each of the following?

- a drink of water
- joining in a ball game
- another helping of potatoes
- watching your favorite TV show
- having your teacher repeat the directions

What have you had to **request** at school? What words can you use to make a polite **request**?

A Word a Day

disaster

noun

A **disaster** is something that turns out all wrong.

It was a **disaster** when we forgot to pick up the cake for the surprise party.

Which of these is a **disaster**?

- a train wreck
- walking a dog
- children singing
- two cars crashing
- buildings falling during an earthquake

Explain how keeping canned food, water, flashlights, a radio, batteries, and blankets in your house can help you be prepared for a **disaster**.

hardship

noun

A **hardship** is a difficult situation.

The first settlers in America faced many **hardships**, including illness and hunger.

Which of the following mean about the same thing as **hardship**?

- difficulty
- surprise
- suffering
- misfortune
- happiness

What other **hardships** did people long ago have to face?

A Word a Day, Primary • EMC 2717 • ©2002 by Evan-Moor Corp.

headquarters

noun

Headquarters is the main office where members of a group meet and decisions are made.

The police officer called **headquarters** to request help from more officers.

Which of the following groups might have **headquarters**?

- babies
- firefighters
- forest rangers
- Girl or Boy Scouts
- cartoon characters

If you were going to form a neighborhood club, where would its **headquarters** be?

reserve

verb

If you arrange to keep something for use at a later time, you **reserve** it.

We called the restaurant to **reserve** a table for dinner tonight.

Which of these could you **reserve**?

- the gas pump at the station
- a place at a summer camp
- a seat on an airplane
- a seat at a ball game
- the bell at school

Why is it a good idea to **reserve** a space ahead of time when you know you're going to have a large group of people?

A Word a Day

route

noun

The path you take to get somewhere is the **route**.

The road was blocked so we had to take another **route** to get to school.

Which of the following mean about the same thing as **route**?

- way
- map
- road
- street
- distance

Describe the shortest **route** from your classroom to the office. Now can you describe a different **route**?

surface

noun

The **surface** is the outer layer of something.

When astronauts landed on the moon, they discovered that the **surface** included chunky rocks and craters.

Which of the following are on the **surface**?

- the roots of a plant
- the seeds of an apple
- an underground tunnel
- butter on a slice of toast
- grass growing on the ground

How is the **surface** of a peach different from the **surface** of an apple?

A Word a Day, Primary • EMC 2717 • ©2002 by Evan-Moor Corp.

task

noun

A **task** is a small job or chore.

My sister's **task** every night is to set the table for dinner.

Which of the following are **tasks**?

- washing the car
- watching a movie
- mowing the lawn
- playing basketball
- sweeping the garage

Tell about the **tasks** you do at home. How often do you do them? Which is your favorite **task**? Which **task** is your least favorite?

healthy

adjective

Someone or something that is in good physical condition is **healthy**.

It's important to get enough sleep if you want to stay **healthy**.

Which of the following are important things to do to stay **healthy**?

- eat junk food
- drink lots of water
- get plenty of exercise
- eat fruits and vegetables
- sit around watching television

What do you do to stay **healthy**? Describe some **healthy** things that you eat and some of the ways you get exercise.

A Word a Day

announce

verb

When you **announce** something, you make a public statement about it.

The birth of my little sister was **announced** in our local paper.

Which of these might be **announced** on the radio or television?

- the winner of the Best Movie of the Year award
- the score of the football game
- the weather for tomorrow
- the time you go to bed
- your phone number

Tell about a time when you or someone in your family had good news to **announce**.

praise

noun

Words that express approval or appreciation are **praise**.

The teacher was full of **praise** for her class for their great performance at the assembly.

Which of the following statements express **praise**?

- "Great job!"
- "Let me help you."
- "That's excellent work!"
- "I think you're going to need to try that again."
- "I love the bright colors you used in that picture!"

Tell about a time when someone gave you a lot of **praise** for something. What was it for? How did the **praise** make you feel about the job you did?

A Word a Day, Primary • EMC 2717 • ©2002 by Evan-Moor Corp.

admire

verb

If you respect and look up to someone, you **admire** him or her.

I **admire** people who can play an instrument.

Which words mean about the same thing as **admire**?

- like
- ignore
- interrupt
- appreciate
- understand

Tell about someone whom you **admire** very much. Why do you **admire** that person? What would you like to be **admired** for some day?

ponder

verb

You **ponder** something when you think about it carefully.

Scientists **ponder** the existence of life on other planets, but no one has proven it yet.

Which of these mean about the same thing as **ponder**?

- study
- refuse
- accept
- examine
- consider

What is something you have **pondered** over? Did you find an answer?

A Word a Day

restrain

verb

When you hold someone back from doing something, you **restrain** him or her.

Joe had to **restrain** his dog so it wouldn't take off and chase the neighbor's cat.

Which of the following mean about the same thing as **restrain**?

- let go
- control
- set free
- pin down
- take control of

Tell about a time when you were very excited about something, but you had to **restrain** your feelings for a while. Was it hard?

zest

noun

If you have energy and enthusiasm, you have **zest**.

The clowns performed with such **zest** that the crowd got excited, too.

Which words describe someone with **zest**?

- lively
- sleepy
- energetic
- bored
- enthusiastic

Do you know someone who is full of **zest**? What is that person like?

enchanted

adjective

If someone or something is **enchanted**, it has been put under a magical spell.

The **enchanted** princess in the story slept for 100 years.

Which of the following might be **enchanted** in a fairy tale?

- a fairy
- a dragon
- a computer
- a talking frog
- a pair of socks

Tell about a favorite story or movie in which there was a character or thing that was **enchanted**. How did the person or thing become **enchanted**? How was the magic spell broken?

doze

verb

When you **doze**, you fall into a light sleep for a short time.

The movie was so boring that I started to **doze** off.

Which of these mean about the same thing as **doze**?

- nap
- study
- snooze
- awaken
- slumber

Where is your favorite place to **doze** on a lazy day?

A Word a Day

hesitate

verb

If you pause for a short time before you do something, you **hesitate**.

Bud **hesitated** a minute before jumping into the cold lake.

If you **hesitate**, would you

- be the first one to answer the question?
- stand for a moment at the corner before crossing?
- volunteer to show a new student around the school?
- wait a few days before going to meet the new neighbors?
- ask your friend to try the food in the cafeteria before you taste it?

Tell about a time when you **hesitated** before doing something. What made you pause? Did you finally go ahead and do it?

optimistic

adjective

An **optimistic** person is always positive about things turning out well.

Even though Jay had a broken arm, he was **optimistic** that it would heal in time for baseball season.

Which statements would an **optimistic** person make?

- "I always have the worst luck."
- "Everything's going to be fine!"
- "Nothing ever works out for me."
- "Tomorrow will be a better day."
- "I know I'm going to feel much better soon!"

Do you know an **optimistic** person? What is he or she like? Do you like being around someone who's **optimistic**? Why?

A Word a Day, Primary • EMC 2717 • ©2002 by Evan-Moor Corp.

disease

noun

A **disease** is a sickness or an illness.

I got a shot to prevent me from getting a **disease** called measles.

Which of these is a **disease**?

- cancer
- freckles
- dimples
- chicken pox
- whooping cough

What do you and your family do to stay healthy and prevent getting a **disease**?

mechanic

noun

A **mechanic** knows all about engines and how they work.

When our car wouldn't start, we took it to a **mechanic** who soon got it running again.

Which of the following might a **mechanic** do?

- fix your sink
- fix an oil leak
- tune up the engine
- repair your computer
- replace the car battery

Would you like to be a **mechanic**? Why or why not?

A Word a Day

recreation
noun

Activities that people do in their free time are called **recreation**.

For **recreation** my dad likes to play tennis on his days off from work.

Which activities would you do for **recreation**?

- go bowling
- mow the lawn
- collect stamps
- play a board game
- clean the bathroom

Tell about activities the people in your family do for **recreation**. What things do you do together for **recreation**?

nourishment
noun

Nourishment is the food that a person, animal, or plant needs to keep healthy.

The newborn puppies got their **nourishment** from their mother's milk.

What would provide **nourishment** for

- you?
- a cat?
- a plant?
- a horse?
- a newborn baby?

Imagine that you're an athlete getting ready to run a big race. What kinds of food do you think would give you the **nourishment** you need?

A Word a Day, Primary • EMC 2717 • ©2002 by Evan-Moor Corp.

persuade

verb

When you convince someone to think or act according to what you say, you **persuade** him or her.

Janie **persuaded** me to choose fruit for dessert because it's healthier than cake.

What would you say to **persuade**

- your brother to turn down his music?
- your parents to let you stay up later?
- your best friend to loan you a game?
- your sister to take your turn doing the dishes?
- your teacher to give you an extra day to do an assignment?

Tell about a time when someone **persuaded** you to do something differently than what you had planned. How did it turn out?

include

verb

When you make someone or something part of a set, you **include** it.

I plan to **include** all my classmates in my birthday celebration.

Which of the following are examples of **including** people?

- choosing people to play on the team
- inviting a friend to work on your group's project
- leaving someone out because you don't like him or her
- encouraging everyone to participate in the science fair
- asking someone to leave the room for being too noisy

Tell about a time when you **included** someone who was alone in an activity. How did being **included** in the group make him or her feel? How did you feel? Have you ever wished that other people would **include** you in something? When?

A Word a Day

insist

verb

You **insist** when you make a demand about something and won't change your mind.

Katie **insisted** on hiking in a dress even though her mother suggested she wear jeans.

Which of the following would you say to **insist** about something?

- "It's really completely up to you."
- "I won't take no for an answer."
- "You absolutely must do it right now."
- "Go ahead and do whatever you choose."
- "You don't have a choice; you have to go."

Tell about a time when someone **insisted** that you do something. How did it make you feel? What is something that you have **insisted** about? Did you get your way?

creative

adjective

A **creative** person uses his or her imagination to come up with new ideas.

My **creative** brother is always thinking up wild stories; he should be a writer.

Which of these mean about the same thing as **creative**?

- dull
- artistic
- talented
- ordinary
- imaginative

In what ways do you like to be **creative**? Do you like to sing, dance, paint, write, play an instrument, or invent things?

A Word a Day, Primary • EMC 2717 • ©2002 by Evan-Moor Corp.

flexible

adjective

If you are **flexible**, you are willing and able to make changes.

Dad can pick us up after school because his schedule is **flexible**.

Which of the following might a **flexible** person say?

- "I can readjust my plans so that everything will work out."
- "I'm open to going to the movies or to miniature golf."
- "The only flavor I want is chocolate."
- "No, I only want to do it my way."
- "Either way is fine with me."

Tell about a time when you were **flexible** and willing to change something you were doing or wanted to do. Why is it important to be **flexible** sometimes?

demolish

verb

If you **demolish** something, you knock it down or destroy it.

The builders had to **demolish** the old library so that they could build a new one.

Which of the following mean about the same thing as **demolish**?

- fix
- ruin
- build
- flatten
- tear down

Which is more exciting: watching a building being built, or watching one getting **demolished**? Why?

A Word a Day

deliberately

adverb

Something done on purpose is done **deliberately**.

Rupert **deliberately** turned up his music while I was reading just to bug me.

Which of the following are probably done **deliberately**?

- crashing into a pole
- tickling your sister
- pushing someone
- stepping on someone's foot
- bumping into someone on a bus

What has someone done **deliberately** to annoy you? How did you react?

coax

verb

When you use gentle words and ways to convince someone to do something, you **coax** him or her.

We used a dish of milk to **coax** the kitten down from the tree.

Which statements would you use to **coax** someone?

- "You're the best!"
- "You'd better, or else."
- "I really appreciate your cooperation."
- "If you don't give it to me, I'll scream."
- "I promise I'll wash dishes for a week if you'll let me go to the party."

Tell about a time when you **coaxed** someone into doing something. What gentle words and ways did you use?

A Word a Day, Primary • EMC 2717 • ©2002 by Evan-Moor Corp.

perspire

verb

When you **perspire**, you sweat.

After you do a lot of exercise and **perspire**, it's a good idea to drink some water.

Which of these might make a person **perspire**?

- running around a track
- lying in a hammock
- working in the sun
- playing baseball
- eating ice cream

What activities make you **perspire**? Why is it important to drink liquids when you are doing something that makes you **perspire**?

ecstatic

adjective

If you're **ecstatic**, you are extremely happy and excited about something.

When our teacher said we were going to space camp, the class became **ecstatic** and started cheering.

Which of the following mean about the same thing as **ecstatic**?

- sad
- thrilled
- delighted
- overjoyed
- unhappy

Tell about a time when you were absolutely **ecstatic** about something. How did that feel? How is being **ecstatic** different from just being happy?

A Word a Day

carpenter

noun

The job of a **carpenter** is to build or fix things made of wood.

My parents hired a **carpenter** to build some bookcases in my bedroom.

Which of these might a **carpenter** do?

- build a desk
- build a house
- decorate a cake
- repair a barn door
- shampoo a carpet

Have you ever watched a **carpenter** work? What tools does a **carpenter** use? If you were a **carpenter**, what would you want to build?

assume

verb

If you **assume**, you decide that something is true without asking or checking it.

I **assumed** it was okay to borrow my sister's shirt, but I was wrong.

Which of the following can you **assume**?

- Rain feels wet.
- We get milk from cows.
- The sun will rise every day.
- You'll always get an A on every paper.
- You'll never have a cold your whole life.

Tell about a time when you got into trouble because you **assumed** something that wasn't correct.

A Word a Day, Primary • EMC 2717 • ©2002 by Evan-Moor Corp.

associate

verb

When we **associate**, we think of things that go together.

We **associate** hearts and flowers with Valentine's Day.

Complete each phrase using the first word you **associate** it with:

- peanut butter and _____

- shoes and _____

- salt and _____

- bread and _____

- ice cream and _____

What are the things that you **associate** with your favorite holiday?

category

noun

A **category** is a group of items that are similar in some way.

Apples, oranges, and kiwis are in the fruit **category**.

Name three items in each of the following **categories**:

- vehicles

- tools

- zoo animals

- buildings

- insects

Pick several items you see in your classroom, and then choose a **category** they all belong in.

A Word a Day

compete

verb

When you **compete**, you are trying to beat others in a race or contest.

My cousin is training to **compete** in a marathon race this summer.

Which of the following are activities that a person might **compete** in?

- a dance performance
- a spelling bee
- a tennis match
- a game of checkers
- an exhibit of paintings

Tell about a time when you **competed** in an activity with a group, a friend, or a relative. Do you like to **compete**? Why or why not?

treacherous

adjective

If something is **treacherous**, it's dangerous.

Skydiving and mountain climbing can be **treacherous** sports.

Which of these signs might you see on a **treacherous** road?

- Danger—Turn Back
- Warning: Icy Roads
- Rest Stop Next Exit
- Windy Road Ahead
- Beautiful View Next Left

Would you like to try a **treacherous** sport someday? Why or why not?

A Word a Day, Primary • EMC 2717 • ©2002 by Evan-Moor Corp.

conceal

verb

When you **conceal** something, you hide it or keep it from being discovered.

I **conceal** my diary in a box under my bed so that no one will read it.

Which words mean about the same thing as **conceal**?

- tell
- cover
- show
- disguise
- display

Tell about a time when you wanted to **conceal** something. How did you manage to keep it from being discovered?

permanent

adjective

Something is **permanent** if it lasts for a very long time or forever.

You should take care of your **permanent** teeth so they don't get cavities.

Which of the following things are **permanent**?

- the ocean
- mountains
- your baby teeth
- being in the first grade
- flowers from your garden

Why is it important to take care of your **permanent** teeth? What could happen if you don't?

A Word a Day

precious

adjective

Something that's valuable and special to you is **precious**.

Our time with Grandma is **precious** because we don't get to see her very often.

Which of these is probably **precious**?

- Grandpa's antique gold watch
- a trunk full of family photos
- a wash rag
- diamonds
- a toy car

Tell about something you have or someone you know that is very **precious** to you.

sluggish

adjective

If you feel **sluggish**, you move slowly and don't have much energy.

After eating a big lunch and resting in the hammock, I felt so **sluggish** that I could barely move.

Which words mean about the same thing as **sluggish**?

- energetic
- tired
- slow
- lively
- sleepy

Tell about a time when you felt **sluggish**. Why did you feel this way, and what did you do to get your energy back? What kinds of things make you feel **sluggish**?

A Word a Day, Primary • EMC 2717 • ©2002 by Evan-Moor Corp.

discussion

noun

When people talk about things, they have a **discussion**.

Our teacher gathered us in a circle for a **discussion** about our next field trip.

Which of the following might you do in a **discussion**?

- take a nap
- listen to other people
- offer your opinion
- ask questions
- brush your teeth

Tell about a time when you had a **discussion** in class or with friends. What was it about? How does a **discussion** help people share their ideas?

advance

verb

When you **advance**, you move forward or make progress.

After I finished the books in Level One, I **advanced** to Level Two.

On a game board, which commands would help a player **advance**?

- "Lose your turn."
- "Move forward to GO."
- "Take another turn!"
- "Move back 3 spaces."
- "Skip ahead 2 spaces."

Tell about a time when you were working on something and got to **advance** to the next level. Why is it important to finish one thing before you **advance** to the next?

A Word a Day

boost

noun

A **boost** is something that lifts you up.

I couldn't reach the doorbell, so my brother gave me a **boost**.

In which of these situations might you need a **boost**?

- when you're feeling sad
- when you're trying to climb a tall tree
- when you're standing on a ladder
- when you can't reach the top shelf
- when you're happy and excited

Tell about a time when someone did or said something that gave you a **boost**. What was something you did to give someone else a **boost**? How did it feel?

barrier

noun

A **barrier** is something that prevents things from going through.

The people made a **barrier** of sandbags to keep the river from flooding their town.

Which of the following could be a **barrier**?

- a brick wall
- an iron gate
- an open field
- a locked door
- the sky

Why are **barriers** set up to block off streets during a parade? In what other situations are **barriers** used?

A Word a Day, Primary • EMC 2717 • ©2002 by Evan-Moor Corp.

recommend

verb

You **recommend** something when you praise its value to others.

I **recommend** the milkshakes at the local diner; they're delicious!

Which of these statements would you use to **recommend** a product?

- "That shampoo got my hair really clean!"
- "This cereal gets soggy so quickly."
- "That movie was so boring it put me to sleep."
- "This game is too complicated."
- "That drink is sweet and delicious!"

Tell about a time when someone **recommended** a book or movie to you. Did you read or see it? What is a book or movie that you have **recommended** to others?

gratitude

noun

Gratitude is a feeling of thankfulness.

When Grandpa gave me his silver watch chain, I showed my **gratitude** by giving him a big hug.

Which statements show **gratitude**?

- "I can't forgive you."
- "You'll get over it soon."
- "I'll always remember this."
- "How can I ever thank you enough?"
- "I really appreciate everything you've done for me."

Tell about a time when you showed **gratitude** for something someone did for you. Tell about a time when someone showed **gratitude** to you for something you did.

A Word a Day

participant

noun

A **participant** is someone who joins in an activity.

All **participants** in the race will receive a T-shirt when they cross the finish line.

Which of these is a **participant**?

- a member of a volleyball team
- a person watching a soccer game
- someone who enters a coloring contest
- someone who writes a letter to a friend
- a member of the cast of the school play

Tell about a time when you were a **participant** in an activity. Then think of a time when you were not a **participant**, but watched others. Which do you think is more fun?

temporary

adjective

Something that lasts only for a short time is **temporary**.

The power outage was **temporary**; our electricity was back on by morning.

Which of the following mean about the same thing as **temporary**?

- momentary
- forever
- changing
- long-lasting
- passing

What was a **temporary** problem you had? How long did it last?

A Word a Day, Primary • EMC 2717 • ©2002 by Evan-Moor Corp.

A Word a Day

purchase

verb

When you **purchase** something, you buy it.

Our family tries to **purchase** things when they're on sale.

Which of the following can you use to **purchase** something?
- a check
- money
- chewing gum
- a credit card
- trading cards

Tell about a time when you **purchased** something with money you earned. How did it feel to **purchase** something with your own money?

ignore

verb

If you **ignore** something, you pay it no attention.

If someone teases you, just **ignore** him or her and walk away.

What might happen if you **ignore**
- your teacher giving you tomorrow's assignment?
- the directions for making something?
- your mom asking for your help?
- someone who is teasing you?
- a Do Not Enter sign?

Tell about a time when you **ignored** someone or something and it was not the right thing to do. Now tell about a time when you **ignored** someone or something because that was the right thing to do.

A Word a Day

decline

verb

When you **decline** something, you turn it down or refuse it.

Mike had to **decline** the invitation to his friend's party because his family was going to be out of town.

Which statements might you make to **decline** something?

- "Thank you, but I'm too full for dessert."
- "I'm sorry, but I won't be able to go."
- "Thank you for that nice invitation."
- "I would love to come over today!"
- "I'm afraid I just can't do that."

Tell about a time when you had to **decline** an invitation. What is a polite way to **decline** an invitation or a request?

plunge

verb

If you dive right into something with a lot of enthusiasm, you **plunge** into it.

I was so eager to start my science project that I **plunged** right into it when I got home from school.

Which of these do you like to **plunge** into?

- homework
- opening presents
- cleaning your room
- eating dessert
- reading your favorite book

Tell about a time when you were so excited about doing something that you **plunged** right into it without anyone telling you to get started. How did that feel?

A Word a Day, Primary • EMC 2717 • ©2002 by Evan-Moor Corp.

capable

verb

If you're able to do something, you're **capable** of doing it.

My brother is **capable** of tying his shoes, but he asks for help anyway.

Which of the following might you be **capable** of doing?

- lifting up a car
- brushing your hair
- pouring a bowl of cereal
- naming all the words in the dictionary
- making your bed

What is something you are **capable** of doing? What is something you want to become **capable** of doing in the future?

massive

adjective

Something that's extraordinarily large, heavy, and solid is **massive**.

It took ten men to move the **massive** oak table into the moving van.

Which of these is **massive**?

- a mountain
- the Statue of Liberty
- a computer mouse
- a light bulb
- a dinosaur

What is the most **massive** thing you have in your house? About how many people would it take to lift it?

A Word a Day

thaw

verb

When something melts after being frozen, it **thaws**.

We let the frozen turkey **thaw** the night before so we could cook it for Thanksgiving dinner.

Which of the following could **thaw**?

- icy streets
- a light bulb
- warm laundry
- a frozen pond or lake
- peas taken out of the freezer

What causes a frozen pond to **thaw**? What can you do to make frozen food **thaw** more quickly?

symphony

noun

A **symphony** is a complicated piece of music played by an orchestra.

The flutes had an important part in the **symphony**.

Which sounds would you probably hear in a **symphony**?

- a cello
- a piano
- banging pots and pans
- a coach's whistle
- a drum

Have you ever listened to a **symphony**? How does the music make you feel? If you could perform a **symphony**, which instrument in the orchestra would you like to play?

A Word a Day, Primary • EMC 2717 • ©2002 by Evan-Moor Corp.

spontaneous

adjective

Something **spontaneous** is done without planning.

I can't make **spontaneous** plans after school; I have to make plans the night before.

Which of the following are examples of **spontaneous** actions?

- A team of climbers scales Mt. Everest.
- A family rushes out after dinner to catch a movie.
- You reserve the skating rink for your birthday party.
- You and your friend decide to switch shoes at recess.
- Your family makes plans during the spring for a summer camping trip.

Do you think a **spontaneous** activity can be more fun than a planned one? Why? What's the advantage of planning ahead of time? What's the advantage of being **spontaneous**?

rickety

adjective

Something **rickety** isn't very strong and could break easily.

The **rickety** old fence blew over with the first strong winter wind.

Which of the following mean about the same thing as **rickety**?

- safe
- shaky
- weak
- wobbly
- unsteady

Why is it a good idea to be careful with something that is **rickety**? Why shouldn't you use something that's **rickety** until it's fixed?

A Word a Day

resource

noun

Someone or something that provides information is a **resource**.

The library is a great **resource** for all sorts of subjects.

Which of the following are **resources** you might find in a library?

- a dictionary
- a world atlas
- a box of cereal
- an encyclopedia
- a grocery store receipt

What kind of **resources** have you used to find information for your schoolwork? How can the people in your family be a **resource** for you?

predicament

noun

A difficult or unpleasant situation is a **predicament**.

The climber was in a **predicament** when his safety rope came loose.

Which of these mean about the same thing as **predicament**?

- a fix
- a jam
- a parade
- a mess
- a contest

Tell about a time when you found yourself in a **predicament**. How did you get out of it?

A Word a Day, Primary • EMC 2717 • ©2002 by Evan-Moor Corp.

perplexed

adjective

If you don't understand something, you're **perplexed**.

I was **perplexed** as I studied the map and read the directions to the museum.

Which words mean about the same thing as **perplexed**?

- sure
- certain
- puzzled
- confused
- unsure

How have you figured out something that you were **perplexed** about? What are some good strategies for understanding something that **perplexes** you?

unruly

adjective

Someone or something **unruly** is hard to control.

The **unruly** crowd went wild when the rock stars appeared.

Which of these mean about the same thing as **unruly**?

- calm
- disorderly
- obedient
- rowdy
- uncontrollable

Have you ever seen someone act **unruly**? How did it make you feel? Why is it important for children not to be **unruly** at school?

A Word a Day

compass

noun

A **compass** is a tool that can help you figure out in which direction you are facing.

We used our **compass** to help us find our way out of the forest.

Which directions would be on a **compass**?

- west
- south
- forward
- northeast
- sideways

In what situations would it be a good idea to have a **compass** with you?

atmosphere

noun

The mood or feeling of a place is its **atmosphere**.

The **atmosphere** at the funeral was quiet and serious.

What kind of **atmosphere** would you expect to find at

- a birthday party?
- the library?
- a football game?
- the circus?
- a hospital?

Describe the **atmosphere** in your classroom right now. How is the **atmosphere** on the playground different from that in the library or classroom?

A Word a Day, Primary • EMC 2717 • ©2002 by Evan-Moor Corp.

collide

verb

When two things crash into each other, they **collide**.

If you don't watch where you're going, you can **collide** with someone.

Which of these might happen when two people **collide**?

- Someone might fall down.
- Someone could win a prize.
- Someone might get a loose tooth.
- Someone could get a good grade.
- Someone could drop what they're carrying.

Tell about a time when you **collided** with someone. Did you get hurt? What can you say to someone when you accidentally **collide** with him or her?

criticize

verb

When you tell someone about what he or she has done wrong, you **criticize**.

Father **criticized** the young child's poor table manners.

Which statements would you make to **criticize** someone?

- "You did a great job."
- "You sure left a big mess when you baked."
- "That's the best story you've ever written!"
- "You didn't take enough time to do that right."
- "You were supposed to come home an hour ago."

Tell about a time when someone **criticized** you. How did you feel? What would be a nice way to **criticize** a person to help him or her make a positive change?

A Word a Day

determined

adjective

When you make a firm decision to do something, you are **determined** to do it.

No matter what anyone else said, Harry was **determined** to finish the race.

Which statements would a **determined** person make?

- "I'm definitely going, and that's all there is to it!"
- "I'm not really sure if I want to do that."
- "I'm happy to do whatever you say."
- "Nothing's going to stop me!"
- "I will win that prize."

What is something you are **determined** to do? How can you make sure you are able to do it?

dilemma

noun

When you have to make a difficult choice, you have a **dilemma**.

Bonnie's **dilemma** was whether to wear her new sweater or her new blouse to the party.

Which of these situations is a **dilemma**?

- You broke your mother's vase and you're afraid to tell her.
- Your friend offers you a choice of one or two chocolates.
- You wore your sister's favorite sweater and tore it.
- You get to choose whether to play in the first or second half of the game.
- Your parents let you choose between a vacation at the beach or in the mountains.

Tell about a time when you faced a **dilemma**. What were the choices you had to make? How did you solve your **dilemma**?

A Word a Day, Primary • EMC 2717 • ©2002 by Evan-Moor Corp.

random

adjective

Something that is **random** does not follow any pattern or order.

The teacher put everyone's name in a hat and chose the teams at **random**.

Which of the following could be in **random** order?

- a calendar
- letters in a word
- names in a phone book
- a list of items in your room
- a list of things to buy at the store

What is something you do each day that can be done in **random** order? What is something that must happen in a particular order?

obvious

adjective

If something is **obvious**, it is very easy to see or understand.

It was **obvious** from the smile on her face that she was happy to see her grandmother.

Which of these mean about the same thing as **obvious**?

- clear
- certain
- doubtful
- unclear
- noticeable

What makes it **obvious** that somebody is upset? What makes it **obvious** that someone is in a good mood?

A Word a Day

obligation

noun

Something that you must do is an **obligation**.

After my birthday, one of my **obligations** is to write thank-you notes to the people who gave me gifts.

Which of the following mean about the same thing as **obligation**?

- job
- wish
- duty
- punishment
- responsibility

Tell about an **obligation** you have at home. Do you have any **obligations** at school? Do you think it's important to honor your **obligations**? Why?

panic

noun

Panic is a sudden feeling of fear that comes over a person or group of people.

I felt **panic** when I got separated from my family in a crowd.

Which of these situations might cause **panic**?

- You get a drink of water.
- A building catches on fire.
- A tiger gets loose at the zoo.
- People picnic peacefully at the park.
- You lock yourself out of your house.

Tell about a time when you felt **panic**. What happened? Why is it a good idea to try and stay calm if you feel **panic**?

A Word a Day, Primary • EMC 2717 • ©2002 by Evan-Moor Corp.

lofty

adjective

Something that is **lofty** is very high, grand, or proud.

The eagle looked down over the entire valley from his **lofty** perch in the trees.

Which of the following could be described as **lofty**?

- the height at which an airplane flies
- a peak in the Rocky Mountains
- the bottom of the ocean
- the top of a skyscraper
- your floor

Have you ever been to a **lofty** place? Where was it? How did you feel up there?

dawdle

verb

When you take extra time to do something, you **dawdle**.

If you **dawdle** before breakfast, you'll miss your ride to school.

Is it a good idea to **dawdle** in each of these situations?

- taking a long bubble bath
- going to a doctor's appointment
- talking to a friend on the phone
- meeting Grandpa's plane at the airport
- getting to a play before the curtain goes up

When do you like to **dawdle**? How do you feel when someone else **dawdles** and you're in a hurry?

A Word a Day

gloomy

adjective

Someone or something **gloomy** is dark and sad.

Soon the dark clouds had turned our sunny picnic into a **gloomy** outing.

Which of the following would you describe as **gloomy**?

- pizza day in the cafeteria
- an underground cavern lit by a flashlight
- your house when the power goes out at sundown
- the way you feel when you learn you got an A on your test
- the way you feel when your field trip is canceled due to snow

What do you do to cheer yourself up when you feel **gloomy**? How can you help cheer up a friend who feels **gloomy**?

ache

noun

An **ache** is a dull, steady pain.

After the doctor gave me a shot, I had an **ache** in my arm for a few days.

Which of these might give you an **ache**?

- eating too many sweets at once
- having a cavity in your tooth
- falling off your bike
- reading a book
- taking a bath

What makes you feel better when you **ache**?

A Word a Day, Primary • EMC 2717 • ©2002 by Evan-Moor Corp.

lackadaisical

adjective

You don't show much interest or enthusiasm for something if you are **lackadaisical** about it.

You probably won't improve too quickly on the piano if you have such a **lackadaisical** attitude about practicing.

Which of the following might you be **lackadaisical** about?

- getting permission to invite your best friend on your family's vacation
- watching a movie being filmed on your street
- seeing a speck of dust on your windowsill
- learning to ride a bike by yourself
- watching a snail crawl

What is something you feel **lackadaisical** about? Is it a good idea to be **lackadaisical** about your schoolwork? Why?

gossip

verb

You **gossip** when you talk about other people's personal matters, whether or not you're sure that what you're saying is the truth.

The neighbors **gossiped** about why the Wong family moved to New York, but no one really knew for sure.

Would you be **gossiping** if you

- told someone the name of your new dog?
- talked about why you didn't like the new girl in class?
- shared a secret your sister told you about her best friend?
- told a friend the new paint color in your bedroom?
- told a story about a child's parents even though you weren't sure it was true?

What could you say to someone who wants to **gossip** about others with you?

A Word a Day

mischief

noun

Mischief is behavior that often annoys or irritates others.

When the puppies chewed up Papi's new slippers, their **mischief** finally got them in trouble.

Which of the following are examples of **mischief**?

- hiding a book from your friend
- doing the dishes without being asked
- tying your friend's shoelaces together
- giving your mother a rose on Mother's Day
- having a pillow fight and getting feathers all over the room

Do you like making **mischief**? How do you feel when someone else makes **mischief**?

moist

adjective

Something that is slightly wet or damp is **moist**.

I used a **moist** towel to wipe the pencil marks off my desk.

Which of these is **moist**?

- the desert
- a leaf after a rainstorm
- warm towels coming out of the dryer
- a sponge after you've squeezed it out
- your bathing suit after you've gone swimming

Do you ever go to bed when your hair is **moist**? How does it look when you wake up?

A Word a Day, Primary • EMC 2717 • ©2002 by Evan-Moor Corp.

adapt

verb

You are able to **adapt** if you can easily fit into all sorts of different situations.

A chameleon can **adapt** to its surroundings by changing color to blend in with rocks and trees.

In which of the following situations would you need to **adapt**?

- moving to a new school in the beginning of the year
- waking up in the same house every day
- having an ice-cream sundae for dessert
- having a new baby in the family
- breaking a leg

Do you **adapt** easily to new situations, or is it hard for you to **adapt**? What helps you to **adapt** and feel comfortable in a new situation?

habitat

noun

A **habitat** is the home to a particular group of plants and animals.

Although you might see a lion at a wild animal park, its natural **habitat** is the African savannah.

What is the natural **habitat** for each of the following?

- ferns
- deer
- seaweed
- polar bears
- howler monkeys

What kind of **habitat** would you like to visit? Where is it?

A Word a Day

drenched

drenched

adjective

When you are **drenched**, you are soaking wet through and through.

We got **drenched** when we were caught out in the rain without an umbrella.

Would you get **drenched** if you were

- standing under a waterfall?
- in your classroom reading?
- sitting at a ball game on a hot day?
- surprised on the shore by a giant wave?
- standing on the lawn when the sprinklers came on?

Tell about a time when you got **drenched**. Was it fun? Did you get cold, or was it a hot day? Was it an accident or on purpose?

absorb

absorb

verb

Something that can **absorb** is able to soak up something.

A heavy-duty sponge can **absorb** even a big puddle of milk.

Which of the following could you **absorb** with a sponge?

- the water in a fish tank
- a mud puddle in your backyard
- water left on the floor after your shower
- grape juice that spilled on the cafeteria floor
- ice cream that melted on the kitchen counter

Do you think it's better to use a rag or a paper towel to **absorb** a spill? Why? Which one is better for the environment?

A Word a Day, Primary • EMC 2717 • ©2002 by Evan-Moor Corp.

legend

noun

A **legend** is a story that is handed down from the past that is usually based on something that really happened.

The **legend** of Johnny Appleseed is based on the life of a man named John Chapman.

Which of these is probably a **legend**?

- Many years ago, dinosaurs roamed the earth.
- My great-uncle Sam could eat fifty pies in one sitting.
- We had a one-legged dog that could run faster than a train.
- My grandmother once stayed up for four days straight sewing a quilt.
- Early settlers crossed the United States in wagons.

If you could have a **legend** passed down about you, what would you like people to say?

glitter

verb

When something **glitters**, it shines and sparkles.

The silver bells look so lovely when they **glitter** in the candlelight.

Which of the following **glitter**?

- a tennis shoe
- a diamond ring
- the stars at night
- jewels in a crown
- a peanut butter sandwich

What is something you own that **glitters**?

A Word a Day

amuse

verb

You **amuse** someone when you make him or her laugh or smile.

The playful monkeys always **amuse** the visitors at the zoo.

Would you be **amused** if

- your new puppy licked your hand?
- a magician found a coin behind your ear?
- someone accidentally stepped on your toe?
- a clown squirted water from a flower pinned to his coat?
- your milk spilled in your lunch and ruined your sandwich?

Tell about a time when someone did something that **amused** you. What is something that you have done to **amuse** others?

weary

adjective

You feel **weary** when you are tired or exhausted.

Mom was **weary** after driving for almost three days to get to Grandma's house.

Which of the following might make you feel **weary**?

- listening to an exciting adventure story
- running around the playground three times
- having a good breakfast before going to school
- staying up until midnight to finish your schoolwork
- carrying a heavy backpack up a steep mountainside

What makes you feel **weary**? What can you do to feel better when you're feeling **weary**?

A Word a Day, Primary • EMC 2717 • ©2002 by Evan-Moor Corp.

A Word a Day

baffled
verb

You are **baffled** when you are confused or puzzled by something.

I was **baffled** by the complicated directions for assembling my new model car.

Which of the following might leave you **baffled**?
- buttoning your shirt
- assembling a puzzle with 100 pieces
- trying to read something in a foreign language
- figuring out which end of the pencil has the eraser
- following directions for folding a piece of paper into a crane

What can you do to get help when you are feeling **baffled** by your work at school or home?

marionette
noun

A **marionette** is a puppet that you can move by pulling its strings.

Pinocchio was a wooden **marionette** until the Blue Fairy helped him become a real live boy.

Which of these describe a **marionette**?
- can be made by hand
- can really walk and talk
- can be a star in the theater
- can be dressed in cute clothing
- can feel sad if people don't like the show

If you had a magical **marionette** that could come to life, what sort of **marionette** would it be?

A Word a Day

command

verb

When you give someone or something orders to follow, you **command** them.

The trainer at the wild animal park **commanded** the wolf to bring him a stick.

Which of the following are **commands**?

- "Go away!"
- "Come here!"
- "That's a nice shirt!"
- "May I borrow your pencil?"
- "Please give me that right now!"

Do you like it when someone **commands** you to do something? Is there a nice way to **command** others?

hilarious

adjective

Something so funny that it makes you laugh is **hilarious**.

The movie was so **hilarious** that we almost cried from laughing so hard.

Which of the following might be **hilarious**?

- changing a light bulb
- a clown at the circus
- watching bread dough rise
- a book of knock-knock jokes
- a puppy chasing its tail

Tell about something **hilarious** that made you laugh.

A Word a Day, Primary • EMC 2717 • ©2002 by Evan-Moor Corp.

devour

verb

When you **devour** something, you eat it very quickly or hungrily.

People like to gather to watch the cheetahs **devour** their steak at feeding time.

Which of these describe something being **devoured**?

- a spider eating a fly
- two ladies eating tea cakes
- a wolf pack eating their prey
- a person eating pies at a pie-eating contest
- a person who was lost in the forest, eating the first meal in days

Have you ever **devoured** some food? If so, what were you eating? Did you enjoy it?

solo

noun

When someone performs music all alone, with no other accompaniment, he or she performs a **solo**.

You could tell that Anoki had been practicing, because he performed his **solo** perfectly.

Which of the following describe a **solo**?

- keeping the beat on a drum while your classmates march
- playing the piano all by yourself at a concert
- singing a song alone as part of a play
- playing on a baseball team
- singing in a choir

Have you ever performed a **solo**? How did you feel, or how do you think you would feel?

A Word a Day

unique

adjective

Someone or something is **unique** if it's the only one of its kind.

A fish that could survive on dry land would be very **unique**.

Which of the following are **unique**?

- white tennis shoes
- a lunch box just like your best friend's
- a planet scientists have never seen before
- the only baseball card ever made of a certain player
- being the only student in the school that has never been absent

What is something about you that is **unique**? What is something **unique** about one of your classmates?

candidate

noun

A **candidate** is someone who is applying for a job or running for office.

Each **candidate** for school president gave a speech at the assembly.

Which of the following are **candidates**?

- the new bus driver
- five people applying for a job
- a new chef at your favorite restaurant
- the people running for president of the United States
- a teacher who visits the school to decide if she wants to accept a job there

Do you think you would ever like to be a **candidate** in an election? Why?

A Word a Day, Primary • EMC 2717 • ©2002 by Evan-Moor Corp.

numerous

adjective

Something is **numerous** if there is a large number of it.

The curious student asked **numerous** questions during the science lesson.

Which of these describe a **numerous** group?

- two goldfish in a bowl
- a family that has one child
- eight friends who go hiking together
- so many toy cars that you can hardly count them
- so many fans at the ball game that every seat is taken

Do you think it's better to have **numerous** friends or **numerous** things? Why?

exact

adjective

If something is **exact**, it is correct and has no mistakes.

We need to know the **exact** measurements of the desk so we can make sure it will fit in my room.

Is it important to be **exact** about

- the letters in words that you spell?
- the time of your dentist appointment?
- the change you receive when shopping?
- the number of leaves on the tree in your yard?
- how many times you blink your eyes each day?

What is something that you are careful to be **exact** about? Why is it important to you?

A Word a Day

digits

noun

Digits are the numerals from zero to nine.

We have started adding numbers with three **digits** in math this week.

Which of the following include **digits**?

- your phone number
- your birth date
- your address
- your name
- your age

Do you have a favorite or lucky **digit**? If so, what is it?

shrub

noun

A **shrub** is a short, woody plant.

The yard looked beautiful now that several of the **shrubs** were blooming.

Which of these is a **shrub**?

- a bush
- a redwood tree
- a pumpkin vine
- a Christmas tree
- a small holly bush

What sort of **shrub** have you seen near your home? Does it ever bloom? When?

A Word a Day, Primary • EMC 2717 • ©2002 by Evan-Moor Corp.

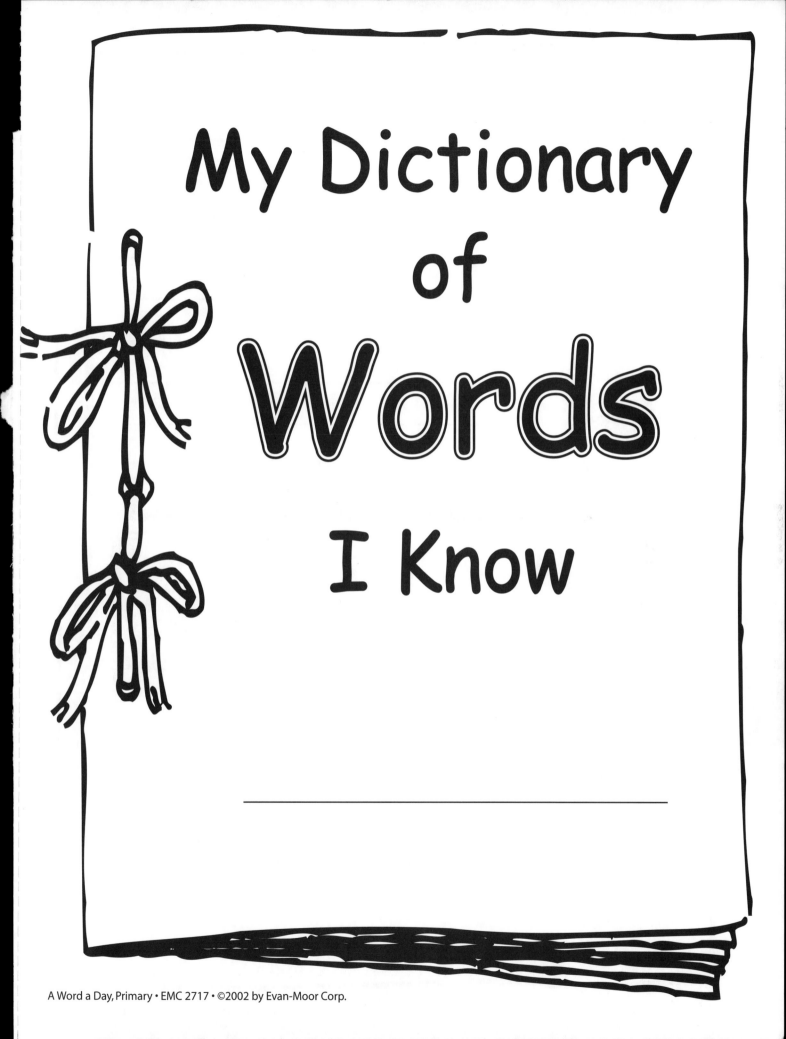

My Dictionary of Words I Know

_____

Word:_____

In my own words:_____

_____

_____

_____

Synonyms:_____

Antonyms:_____

Picture This!

_____

_____

Index

190

A Word a Day, Primary • EMC 2717 • ©2002 by Evan-Moor Corp.